CONTENTS

D1466034

Cookie Jar Favorite

CRISPY'S IRRESISTIBLE PEANUT BUTTER MARBLES

1 package (18 ounces) refrigerated peanut butter cookie dough
2 cups "M&M's"® Milk Chocolate Mini Baking Bits, divided
1 cup crisp rice cereal, divided (optional)
1 package (18 ounces) refrigerated sugar cookie dough
¼ cup unsweetened cocoa powder

In large bowl combine peanut butter dough, 1 cup "M&M's"® Milk Chocolate Mini Baking Bits and ½ cup cereal, if desired. Remove dough to small bowl; set aside. In large bowl combine sugar dough and cocoa powder until well blended. Stir in remaining 1 cup "M&M's"® Milk Chocolate Mini Baking Bits and remaining ½ cup cereal, if desired. Remove half the dough to small bowl; set aside. Combine half the peanut butter dough with half the chocolate dough by folding together just enough to marble. Shape marbled dough into 8×2-inch log. Wrap log in plastic wrap. Repeat with remaining doughs. Refrigerate logs 2 hours. To bake, preheat oven to 350°F. Cut dough into ¼-inch-thick slices. Place about 2 inches apart on ungreased cookie sheets. Bake 12 to 14 minutes. Cool 1 minute on cookie sheets; cool completely on wire racks. Store in tightly covered container.

Makes 5 dozen cookies

CRISPY'S IRRESISTIBLE PEANUT BUTTER MARBLES

Choco-Orange Macadamia Cookies

1 cup raw macadamia nuts
2 cups plus 1 tablespoon all-purpose flour
½ teaspoon baking powder
½ teaspoon salt
¾ cup (1½ sticks) butter, melted and cooled
1 cup packed light brown sugar
6 tablespoons granulated sugar
2 teaspoons grated orange peel
2 teaspoons vanilla
1 egg
1 egg yolk
1 cup (6 ounces) semisweet chocolate chips
½ cup flaked coconut

1. Preheat oven to 350°F. Line cookie sheets with parchment paper or leave ungreased. Set aside.

2. Place macadamia nuts on ungreased shallow baking pan. Bake 8 to 10 minutes or until golden brown and fragrant, stirring frequently. (Nuts can easily burn so watch carefully.) Cool completely. Coarsely chop nuts; reserve.

3. Combine flour, baking powder and salt in medium bowl.

4. Beat butter, sugars, orange peel and vanilla with electric mixer on medium speed until creamy. Beat in egg and egg yolk until fluffy. Gradually add flour mixture, beating until just blended. Stir in nuts, chocolate chips and coconut.

5. Drop dough by rounded tablespoonfuls 2 inches apart onto prepared cookie sheets. Bake 10 to 12 minutes or until edges are just brown but centers are pale. Cool on cookie sheets 1 minute. Remove to wire racks; cool completely. Store in airtight container. *Makes about 3 dozen cookies*

CHOCO-ORANGE MACADAMIA COOKIES

REESE'S® PEANUT BUTTER AND MILK CHOCOLATE CHIP STUDDED OATMEAL COOKIES

1 cup (2 sticks) butter or margarine, softened
1 cup packed light brown sugar
⅓ cup granulated sugar
2 eggs
1½ teaspoons vanilla extract
1½ cups all-purpose flour
1 teaspoon baking soda
½ teaspoon salt
½ teaspoon ground cinnamon (optional)
2½ cups quick-cooking oats
1¾ cups (11-ounce package) REESE'S® Peanut Butter and Milk Chocolate Chips

1. Heat oven to 350°F.

2. Beat butter, brown sugar and granulated sugar in bowl until creamy. Add eggs and vanilla; beat well. Combine flour, baking soda, salt and cinnamon, if desired; add to butter mixture, beating well. Stir in oats and chips (batter will be stiff). Drop by rounded teaspoons onto ungreased cookie sheet.

3. Bake 10 to 12 minutes or until lightly browned. Cool 1 minute; remove from cookie sheet to wire rack.   *Makes about 4 dozen cookies*

Bar Variation: Spread batter into lightly greased 13×9×2-inch baking pan or 15½×10½×1-inch jelly-roll pan. Bake at 350°F. for 20 to 25 minutes or until golden brown. Cool; cut into bars. Makes about 3 dozen bars.

REESE'S® PEANUT BUTTER AND MILK CHOCOLATE CHIP STUDDED OATMEAL COOKIES

GRANDMA'S OLD-FASHIONED OATMEAL COOKIES

2 cups sugar
1 cup shortening
2 eggs
3½ cups all-purpose flour
3 cups uncooked old-fashioned oats
1 teaspoon baking soda
1 teaspoon salt
1 teaspoon ground cinnamon
1 cup buttermilk
1 cup raisins

1. Preheat oven to 350°F. Lightly grease cookie sheets.

2. Combine sugar and shortening in large bowl. Beat with electric mixer at medium speed until creamy. Beat in eggs, one at a time, until mixture is light and fluffy.

3. Combine flour, oats, baking soda, salt and cinnamon in separate bowl. Beat into shortening mixture, one third at a time, alternating with buttermilk until well blended. Stir in raisins.

4. Drop dough by rounded tablespoonfuls onto prepared cookie sheets. Bake 12 to 15 minutes or until lightly browned. Cool slightly on cookie sheets. Remove to wire racks; cool completely. Store at room temperature in airtight containers.   *Makes 4 to 5 dozen cookies*

GRANDMA'S OLD-FASHIONED OATMEAL COOKIES

PRIZED PEANUT BUTTER CRUNCH COOKIES

1 CRISCO® Butter Flavor Stick or 1 cup CRISCO® Butter Flavor Shortening
2 cups firmly packed brown sugar
1 cup JIF® Extra Crunchy Peanut Butter
4 egg whites, lightly beaten
1 teaspoon vanilla
2 cups PILLSBURY BEST® All-Purpose Flour
1 teaspoon baking soda
½ teaspoon baking powder
2 cups crisp rice cereal
1½ cups chopped peanuts
1 cup quick oats (not instant or old-fashioned)
1 cup flake coconut

1. Heat oven to 350°F. Place sheets of foil on countertop for cooling cookies.

2. Combine CRISCO Shortening, sugar and peanut butter in large bowl. Beat at medium speed of electric mixer until blended. Beat in egg whites and vanilla.

3. Combine flour, baking soda and baking powder. Beat into creamed mixture at low speed until just blended. Stir in, one at a time, rice cereal, nuts, oats and coconut with spoon.

4. Drop rounded measuring tablespoonfuls of dough 2 inches apart onto ungreased baking sheet.

5. Bake at 350°F, one baking sheet at a time, for 8 to 10 minutes or until set. *Do not overbake.* Remove cookies to foil to cool completely.

Makes about 4 dozen cookies

White Chocolate Biggies

1½ cups (3 sticks) butter, softened
1 cup granulated sugar
¾ cup packed light brown sugar
2 eggs
2 teaspoons vanilla
2½ cups all-purpose flour
⅔ cup unsweetened cocoa powder
1 teaspoon baking soda
½ teaspoon salt
1 package (10 ounces) large white chocolate chips *or* 1 white chocolate bar, chopped
¾ cup pecan halves, coarsely chopped
½ cup golden raisins

1. Preheat oven to 350°F. Lightly grease cookie sheets or line with parchment paper.

2. Beat butter, sugars, eggs and vanilla in large bowl until light and fluffy. Combine flour, cocoa, baking soda and salt in medium bowl; blend into butter mixture until smooth. Stir in white chocolate chips, pecans and raisins.

3. Drop dough by ⅓ cupfuls onto prepared cookie sheets, spacing about 4 inches apart. Press each cookie to flatten slightly.

4. Bake 12 to 14 minutes or until firm in center. Cool 5 minutes on cookie sheets; remove to wire racks to cool completely.

Makes about 2 dozen cookies

CHOCOLATE CHIP COOKIES

2½ CRISCO® Sticks or 2½ cups CRISCO® Shortening
3¾ cups brown sugar
  ⅓ cup milk
  3 eggs
  2 tablespoons vanilla
5½ cups PILLSBURY BEST® All-Purpose Flour
  1 tablespoon salt
  2 teaspoons baking soda
  3 cups chocolate chips

In the bowl of an electric mixer, cream CRISCO Shortening and brown sugar. Add milk, eggs and vanilla; mix until well blended. In a large mixing bowl, combine PILLSBURY BEST® Flour, salt and baking soda; add to creamed mixture Stir to combine. By hand, stir in chocolate chips. Drop mixture by rounded spoonfuls 2 inches apart onto ungreased baking sheets. Bake 8 to 10 minutes or until lightly golden brown. Cool on pans on wire racks.

Makes 5 dozen cookies

Prep Time: 15 minutes
Bake Time: 8 to 10 minutes

Baking Tips

Most cookies should be removed from cookie sheets immediately after baking and placed in a single layer on wire racks to cool. Fragile cookies may need to cool slightly on the cookie sheet before being moved.

CHOCOLATE CHIP COOKIES

COCONUT MACAROONS

1 (14-ounce) can EAGLE BRAND® Sweetened Condensed Milk (NOT evaporated milk)
1 egg white
2 teaspoons vanilla extract
1 to 1½ teaspoons almond extract
2 (7-ounce) packages flaked coconut (5⅓ cups)

1. Preheat oven to 325°F. Line baking sheets with foil; grease and flour foil. Set aside.

2. In large bowl, combine EAGLE BRAND®, egg white, vanilla and almond extract. Stir in coconut. Drop by rounded teaspoonfuls onto prepared baking sheets; with spoon, slightly flatten each mound.

3. Bake 15 to 17 minutes or until golden. Remove from baking sheets; cool on wire racks. Store loosely covered at room temperature.

Makes about 4 dozen cookies

Prep Time: 10 minutes
Bake Time: 15 to 17 minutes

COCONUT MACAROONS

PEANUT BUTTER JUMBOS

½ cup (1 stick) butter, softened
1½ cups peanut butter
1 cup granulated sugar
1 cup packed brown sugar
3 eggs
2 teaspoons baking soda
1 teaspoon vanilla
4½ cups uncooked old-fashioned oats
1 cup (6 ounces) semisweet chocolate chips
1 cup candy-coated chocolate pieces

1. Preheat oven to 350°F. Lightly grease cookie sheets or line with parchment paper.

2. Beat butter, peanut butter, sugars and eggs in large bowl until well blended. Blend in baking soda, vanilla and oats until well mixed. Stir in chocolate chips and candy pieces.

3. Scoop out about ⅓ cup dough for each cookie. Place on prepared cookie sheets, spacing about 4 inches apart. Press each cookie to flatten slightly. Bake 15 to 20 minutes or until firm in center. Remove to wire racks to cool.   *Makes about 1½ dozen cookies*

Peanut Butter Jumbo Sandwiches: Prepare cookies as directed. Place ⅓ cup softened chocolate or vanilla ice cream on cookie bottom. Top with another cookie. Lightly press sandwich together. Repeat with remaining cookies. Wrap sandwiches in plastic wrap; freeze until firm.

BUTTER TOFFEE CHOCOLATE CHIP CRUNCH

   1 cup firmly packed light brown sugar
   ¾ **CRISCO® Butter Flavor Stick or ¾ cup CRISCO® Butter Flavor Shortening**
      plus additional for greasing
   1 egg
   2 tablespoons sweetened condensed milk (not evaporated milk)
   1 teaspoon salt
   ¾ teaspoon baking soda
   1 teaspoon vanilla
1¾ cups **PILLSBURY BEST® All-Purpose Flour**
   ¾ cup coarsely chopped pecans
   ½ cup milk chocolate chips
   ½ cup semisweet chocolate chips
   2 to 4 bars (1.4 ounces each) toffee bars, finely crushed

1. Heat oven to 350°F. Grease baking sheet with CRISCO Shortening. Place sheets of foil on countertop for cooling cookies.

2. Combine brown sugar, ¾ stick CRISCO Shortening, egg, sweetened condensed milk, salt, baking soda and vanilla in large bowl. Beat at medium speed of electric mixer until well blended. Add flour gradually at low speed. Beat until well blended. Stir in nuts, milk chocolate chips, semisweet chocolate chips and crushed toffee bars with spoon. Drop by level measuring tablespoonfuls 2 inches apart onto prepared baking sheet.

3. Bake at 350°F for 10 to 12 minutes or until light golden brown. *Do not overbake.* Cool 2 minutes on baking sheet. Remove cookies to foil to cool completely.   *Makes about 4 dozen cookies*

CHOCOLATE CHIP-OAT COOKIES

> 1 package (18¼ ounces) yellow cake mix
> 1 teaspoon baking powder
> ¾ cup vegetable oil
> 2 eggs
> 1 teaspoon vanilla
> 1 cup uncooked old-fashioned oats
> ¾ cup semisweet chocolate chips

1. Preheat oven to 350°F. Lightly grease cookie sheets or line with parchment paper.

2. Stir together cake mix and baking powder in large bowl. Add oil, eggs and vanilla; beat by hand until well blended. Stir in oats and chocolate chips.

3. Drop dough by slightly rounded tablespoonfuls 2 inches apart onto prepared cookie sheets. Bake 10 minutes or until golden brown. *Do not overbake.*

4. Let cookies stand on cookie sheets 5 minutes; transfer to wire racks to cool completely.   *Makes 4 dozen cookies*

Baking Tips

Heavy aluminum cookie sheets produce the most evenly baked and browned cookies. Dark sheets can cause over browning and burnt bottoms. Cookies won't get as crisp if you bake them on insulated sheets— the ones with an air pocket —and may take slightly longer to cook.

CHOCOLATE CHIP-OAT COOKIES

PEPPERMINT PATTIES

2 cups all-purpose flour
½ cup plus 1 tablespoon unsweetened cocoa powder, sifted, divided
1 teaspoon baking powder
½ teaspoon salt
¾ cup (1½ sticks) butter, softened
1 cup granulated sugar
1 egg
4 teaspoons vanilla, divided
1 teaspoon pure peppermint extract
3 cups powdered sugar
4 tablespoons hot water or milk (not boiling)

1. Combine flour, ½ cup cocoa, baking powder and salt in small bowl; set aside. Combine butter and granulated sugar in large bowl. Beat with electric mixer at medium speed 1 minute or until creamy. Add egg, 1 teaspoon vanilla and peppermint extract; beat until well blended. Gradually stir in flour mixture just until blended.

2. On lightly floured work surface, shape dough into 12×2-inch log. Wrap tightly in waxed paper, then wrap in plastic wrap. Freeze 2 hours or until firm.

3. Preheat oven to 350°F. Grease cookie sheets. Cut dough into ⅛-inch slices. Place slices 1 inch apart on prepared cookie sheets. Bake 9 minutes or until puffed and firm to the touch. Cool on cookie sheets 1 to 2 minutes. Transfer to wire racks to cool completely.

4. For icing, combine powdered sugar, hot water and remaining 3 teaspoons vanilla in medium bowl; stir until smooth. Add additional water, ½ teaspoon at a time, if necessary, until desired consistency is reached. Divide icing in half. Add remaining 1 tablespoon cocoa powder to one bowl; stir until well blended. Cover cocoa icing; set aside.

5. Frost cooled cookies with vanilla icing; let stand until set. Drizzle cookies with chocolate icing; let stand until set. *Makes about 4 dozen cookies*

PEPPERMINT PATTIES

CHOCOLATE CHERRY COOKIES

1 package (8 ounces) chocolate cake mix
3 tablespoons fat-free (skim) milk
½ teaspoon almond extract
10 maraschino cherries, rinsed, drained and cut into halves
2 tablespoons white chocolate chips
½ teaspoon canola oil

1. Preheat oven to 350°F. Spray cookie sheets with nonstick cooking spray; set aside.

2. Combine cake mix, milk and almond extract in medium bowl. Beat with electric mixer at low speed. Increase speed to medium when mixture looks crumbly; beat 2 minutes or until smooth dough forms. (Dough will be very sticky.)

3. Coat hands with cooking spray. Shape dough into 1-inch balls. Place balls 2½ inches apart on prepared cookie sheets. Flatten each ball slightly. Place cherry half in center of each cookie.

4. Bake 8 to 9 minutes or until cookies lose their shininess and tops begin to crack. *Do not overbake.* Remove to wire racks; cool completely.

5. Place white chocolate chips and oil in small microwavable bowl. Microwave at HIGH 30 seconds; stir. Repeat as necessary until chips are melted and mixture is smooth. Drizzle white chocolate mixture over cookies. Let stand until set.   *Makes about 2 dozen cookies*

CHOCOLATE CHERRY COOKIES

HERSHEY'S TRIPLE CHOCOLATE COOKIES

**48 HERSHEY'S KISSES® Brand Milk Chocolates or HERSHEY'S KISSES® Brand
   WITH ALMONDS Chocolates**
½ cup (1 stick) butter or margarine, softened
¾ cup granulated sugar
¾ cup packed light brown sugar
1 teaspoon vanilla extract
2 eggs
1 tablespoon milk
2¼ cups all-purpose flour
⅓ cup HERSHEY'S Cocoa
1 teaspoon baking soda
½ teaspoon salt
1 cup HERSHEY'S Semi-Sweet Chocolate Chips

1. Remove wrappers from chocolates. Heat oven to 350°F.

2. Beat butter, granulated sugar, brown sugar and vanilla with electric mixer on medium speed in large bowl until well blended. Add eggs and milk; beat well.

3. Stir together flour, cocoa, baking soda and salt; gradually beat into butter mixture, beating until well blended. Stir in chocolate chips. Shape dough into 1-inch balls. Place on ungreased cookie sheet.

4. Bake 10 to 11 minutes or until set. Gently press a chocolate into center of each cookie. Remove to wire rack and cool completely.

Makes about 4 dozen cookies

Variation: For vanilla cookies, omit cocoa and add an additional ⅓ cup all-purpose flour.

HERSHEY's TRIPLE CHOCOLATE COOKIES

BEST EVER PEANUT BUTTER-OATMEAL COOKIES

2 cups quick cooking oats

2 cups all-purpose flour

1 teaspoon baking powder

1 teaspoon baking soda

¼ teaspoon salt

1 cup (2 sticks) SHEDD'S® Spread Country Crock Spread-Stick

1 cup SKIPPY® Creamy or Super Chunk® Peanut Butter

1 cup sugar

1 cup firmly packed brown sugar

2 eggs

2 teaspoons vanilla extract

1 package (12 ounces) semi-sweet chocolate chips (optional)

1. Preheat oven to 350°F. In small bowl, combine oats, flour, baking powder, baking soda and salt; set aside.

2. In large bowl, with electric mixer on medium speed, beat Country Crock and peanut butter until smooth. Beat in sugars, then eggs and vanilla until blended. Beat in flour mixture just until blended, then stir in chocolate chips.

3. On ungreased baking sheets, drop dough by rounded tablespoonfuls, 2 inches apart.

4. Bake 13 minutes or until golden. Remove cookies to wire rack and cool completely.

Makes about 6 dozen cookies

Prep Time: 20 minutes
Bake Time: 13 minutes

CHIPPY CHOCOLATE PEANUT BUTTER COOKIES

5½ cups all-purpose flour
2 teaspoons baking soda
2 teaspoons salt
2 cups (4 sticks) margarine, softened
1½ cups granulated sugar
1½ cups packed light brown sugar
2 teaspoons vanilla
1 teaspoon water
4 eggs
1 package (12 ounces) semisweet chocolate chips
1 package (12 ounces) peanut butter chips

1. Combine flour, baking soda and salt in medium bowl; set aside.

2. Combine margarine, sugars, vanilla and water in large bowl. Beat with electric mixer at medium speed until creamy. Add eggs, one at a time, mixing well after each addition. Add flour mixture in 2 additions, beating at low speed until stiff dough forms. Stir in chocolate and peanut butter chips. Cover; refrigerate 1 hour.

3. Preheat oven to 350°F.

4. Shape teaspoonfuls of dough into smooth balls; place on ungreased cookie sheets. Bake 8 to 10 minutes or until golden brown. Cool on cookie sheets 1 minute. Remove to wire racks; cool completely.

Makes about 6 dozen cookies

CHOCOLATE CHIP TREASURE COOKIES

1½ cups graham cracker crumbs
½ cup all-purpose flour
2 teaspoons baking powder
1 (14-ounce) can EAGLE BRAND® Sweetened Condensed Milk (NOT evaporated milk)
½ cup (1 stick) butter or margarine, softened
1⅓ cups flaked coconut
1 (12-ounce) package semisweet chocolate chips
1 cup chopped walnuts

1. Preheat oven to 375°F. In small bowl, combine graham cracker crumbs, flour and baking powder.

2. In large bowl, beat EAGLE BRAND® and butter until smooth. Add crumb mixture; mix well. Stir in coconut, chocolate chips and walnuts.

3. Drop by rounded tablespoonfuls onto ungreased baking sheets. Bake 9 to 10 minutes or until lightly browned. Cool. Store loosely covered at room temperature.

Makes about 3 dozen cookies

Prep Time: 15 minutes
Bake Time: 9 to 10 minutes

CHOCOLATE CHIP TREASURE COOKIES

CHOCOLATE PEANUT BUTTER CHIP COOKIES

8 (1-ounce) squares semisweet chocolate
3 tablespoons butter or margarine
1 (14-ounce) can EAGLE BRAND® Sweetened Condensed Milk
   (NOT evaporated milk)
2 cups biscuit baking mix
1 egg
1 teaspoon vanilla extract
1 cup (6 ounces) peanut butter chips

1. Preheat oven to 350°F. In large saucepan over low heat, melt chocolate and butter with EAGLE BRAND®; remove from heat. Add biscuit mix, egg and vanilla; with mixer, beat until smooth and well blended.

2. Let mixture cool to room temperature. Stir in peanut butter chips. Shape into 1¼-inch balls. Place 2 inches apart on ungreased baking sheets. Bake 6 to 8 minutes or until tops are lightly crusty. Cool. Store tightly covered at room temperature. *Makes about 4 dozen cookies*

Prep Time: 15 minutes
Bake Time: 6 to 8 minutes

Baking Tips

Never store two kinds of cookies in
the same container, because their
flavors and textures can change.

CHOCOLATE PEANUT BUTTER CHIP COOKIES

MOCHA LATTE THINS

⅓ **cup all-purpose flour**
⅛ **teaspoon salt**
¾ **cup sugar**
½ **cup (1 stick) plus 1 tablespoon unsalted butter, softened, divided**
 2 **eggs**
1½ **teaspoons vanilla**
 2 **tablespoons instant espresso powder, dissolved in 2 tablespoons hot water**
 3 **(3½-ounce) bars bittersweet chocolate, finely chopped**
¼ **cup white chocolate chips**

1. Sift together flour and salt; set aside. Combine sugar and ½ cup butter in large bowl. Beat with electric mixer at medium speed until creamy. Add eggs and vanilla; beat until smooth. Stir in espresso mixture. (There will be some extra grounds that will not dissolve. Do not stir in.)

2. Add flour mixture to butter mixture; beat just until blended. Stir in bittersweet chocolate. Refrigerate dough at least 2 hours or overnight.

3. Preheat oven to 350°F. Line cookie sheets with parchment paper; grease paper. Drop by level teaspoonfuls about 1 inch apart, 20 to a pan. (Dough will still be sticky and may require some molding with fingers.) Bake 7 to 8 minutes or until lightly browned.

4. Let cookies cool on cookie sheets 1 minute. Transfer to wire racks; cool completely.

5. Combine white chocolate chips and remaining 1 tablespoon butter in microwavable bowl. Microwave on HIGH 50 seconds; stir well. If necessary, microwave at additional 10-second intervals until chocolate is completely melted when stirred. Drizzle white chocolate from tip of spoon onto cooled cookies.   *Makes about 8 dozen thins*

Note: Cookies are very crisp when first baked. They become softer after a few hours. Store in tightly covered container.

MOCHA LATTE THINS

QUICK FRUIT & LEMON DROPS

½ cup sugar
1 package (18¼ ounces) lemon cake mix
⅓ cup water
¼ cup (½ stick) butter, softened
1 egg
1 tablespoon grated lemon peel
1 cup mixed dried fruit bits

1. Preheat oven to 350°F. Grease cookie sheets. Place sugar in shallow bowl.

2. Combine cake mix, water, butter, egg and lemon peel in large bowl. Beat with electric mixer at low speed until well blended. Beat in fruit bits just until blended.

3. Shape dough by heaping tablespoonfuls into balls; roll in sugar to coat. Place 2 inches apart on prepared cookie sheets.

4. Bake 12 to 14 minutes or until set. Let cookies stand on cookie sheets 2 minutes; transfer to wire racks to cool completely.

Makes about 2 dozen cookies

Note: If dough is too sticky to handle, add about ¼ cup all-purpose flour.

QUICK FRUIT & LEMON DROPS

Chockful of Chips

CINNAMON CHIPS GEMS

    1 cup (2 sticks) butter or margarine, softened
    2 packages (3 ounces each) cream cheese, softened
    2 cups all-purpose flour
    ½ cup sugar
    ⅓ cup ground toasted almonds
    2 eggs
    1 can (14 ounces) sweetened condensed milk
    1 teaspoon vanilla extract
    1⅓ cups HERSHEY᛬S Cinnamon Chips, divided

1. Beat butter and cream cheese in large bowl until well blended; stir in flour, sugar and almonds. Cover; refrigerate about 1 hour.

2. Divide dough into 4 equal parts. Shape each part into 12 smooth balls. Place each ball in small muffin cup (1¾ inches in diameter); press evenly on bottom and up side of each cup.

3. Heat oven to 375°F. Beat eggs in small bowl. Add sweetened condensed milk and vanilla; mix well. Place 7 cinnamon chips in bottom of each cookie shell; fill a generous three-fourths full with sweetened condensed milk mixture.

4. Bake 18 to 20 minutes or until tops are puffed and just beginning to turn golden brown. Cool 3 minutes. Sprinkle about 15 chips on top of each cookie. Cool completely in pan on wire rack. Remove from pan using small metal spatula or sharp knife. Store tightly covered at room temperature.

Makes 4 dozen cookies

CINNAMON CHIPS GEMS

TOFFEE CHIPSTERS

1 package (18 ounces) refrigerated sugar cookie dough
1 cup white chocolate chips
1 bag (8 ounces) chocolate-covered toffee baking bits, divided

1. Preheat oven to 350°F. Lightly grease cookie sheets. Let dough stand at room temperature about 15 minutes.

2. Combine dough, white chocolate chips and 1 cup toffee bits in large bowl; beat until well blended. Drop dough by rounded tablespoonfuls 2 inches apart onto prepared cookie sheets. Press remaining ⅓ cup toffee bits into dough mounds.

3. Bake 10 to 12 minutes or until set. Cool on cookie sheets 1 minute. Remove to wire racks; cool completely. *Makes about 2 dozen cookies*

Baking Tips

Most cookies freeze well for several months. Store unfrosted cookies in sealed plastic bags or airtight containers with plastic wrap or waxed paper between layers of cookies. Most cookies thaw at room temperature in 10 to 15 minutes.

TOFFEE CHIPSTERS

DOUBLE CHOCOLATE CRANBERRY CHUNKIES

1¾ cups all-purpose flour
⅓ cup unsweetened cocoa powder
½ teaspoon baking powder
½ teaspoon salt
1 cup (2 sticks) butter, softened
1 cup granulated sugar
½ cup packed brown sugar
1 egg
1 teaspoon vanilla
2 cups semisweet chocolate chunks or large chocolate chips
¾ cup dried cranberries or dried tart cherries
Additional granulated sugar

1. Preheat oven to 350°F.

2. Combine flour, cocoa, baking powder and salt in small bowl; set aside. Combine butter, 1 cup granulated sugar and brown sugar in large bowl. Beat with electric mixer at medium speed until light and fluffy. Beat in egg and vanilla until well blended. Gradually beat in flour mixture at low speed until blended. Stir in chocolate chunks and cranberries.

3. Drop dough by level ¼ cupfuls onto ungreased cookie sheets, spacing 3 inches apart. Flatten dough until 2½ inches in diameter with bottom of glass that has been dipped in additional granulated sugar.

4. Bake 11 to 12 minutes or until cookies are set. Cool cookies 2 minutes on cookie sheets; transfer to wire racks. Cool completely.

Makes about 1 dozen (4-inch) cookies

Tip: To make smaller cookies, drop dough by tablespoonfuls onto ungreased cookie sheets, spacing 2 inches apart. Flatten dough until 1½ inches in diameter as directed in step 3. Bake cookies for 10 to 11 minutes or until set. Makes 3 dozen (2½ inch) cookies.

DOUBLE CHOCOLATE CRANBERRY CHUNKIES

DARK CHOCOLATE DREAMS

16 ounces bittersweet chocolate candy bars or bittersweet chocolate chips
¼ cup (½ stick) butter
½ cup all-purpose flour
¾ teaspoon ground cinnamon
½ teaspoon baking powder
¼ teaspoon salt
1½ cups sugar
3 eggs
1 teaspoon vanilla
1 package (12 ounces) white chocolate chips
1 cup chopped pecans, lightly toasted

1. Preheat oven to 350°F. Grease cookie sheets.

2. Coarsely chop chocolate bars; place in large microwavable bowl. Add butter. Microwave at HIGH 2 minutes; stir. Microwave 1 to 2 minutes, stirring after 1 minute, or until chocolate is melted. Let cool slightly.

3. Combine flour, cinnamon, baking powder and salt in small bowl; set aside.

4. Combine sugar, eggs and vanilla in medium bowl. Beat with electric mixer at medium-high speed about 6 minutes or until very thick and mixture turns pale in color. Reduce speed to low; slowly beat in chocolate mixture until well blended. Gradually beat in flour mixture until blended. Fold in white chocolate chips and pecans.

5. Drop dough by level ⅓ cupfuls onto prepared cookie sheets, spacing 3 inches apart. Place piece of plastic wrap over dough; flatten dough with fingertips to form 4-inch circles. Remove plastic wrap.

6. Bake 12 minutes or until just firm to the touch and surface begins to crack. *Do not overbake.* Cool cookies 2 minutes on cookie sheets. Remove to wire racks to cool completely.   *Makes 10 to 12 (5-inch) cookies*

Note: Cookies can be baked on ungreased cookie sheets lined with parchment paper. Cool cookies 2 minutes on cookie sheets; slide parchment paper and cookies onto countertop. Cool completely.

DARK CHOCOLATE DREAMS

Moon Rocks

1 package (18¼ ounces) devil's food or German chocolate cake mix with pudding in the mix

3 eggs

½ cup (1 stick) butter, melted

2 cups slightly crushed (2½-inch) pretzel sticks

1½ cups uncooked old-fashioned oats

1 cup swirled chocolate and white chocolate chips or candy-coated semisweet chocolate baking pieces

1. Preheat oven to 350°F. Blend cake mix, eggs and butter in large bowl. Stir in crushed pretzels, oats and chocolate chips. (Dough will be stiff.)

2. Drop dough by rounded teaspoonfuls about 2 inches apart onto ungreased cookie sheets.

3. Bake 7 to 9 minutes or until set. Let cookies cool on cookie sheets 1 minute; transfer to wire racks to to cool completely.

Makes about 5 dozen cookies

Baking Tips

Cool individual cookies on a wire rack. If the cookies seem too tender or begin to fall apart when removed from the pan, allow them to cool a minute or two before transferring to the cooling rack.

MOON ROCKS

CHOCOLATE MACADAMIA CHIPPERS

1 package (18 ounces) refrigerated chocolate chip cookie dough
3 tablespoons unsweetened cocoa powder
½ cup coarsely chopped macadamia nuts
  Powdered sugar (optional)

1. Preheat oven to 375°F. Let dough stand at room temperature about 15 minutes.

2. Combine dough and cocoa in large bowl; beat until well blended. (Dough may be kneaded lightly, if desired.) Stir in nuts. Drop by heaping tablespoons 2 inches apart onto ungreased cookie sheets.

3. Bake 9 to 11 minutes or until almost set. Transfer to wire racks to cool completely. Dust lightly with powdered sugar, if desired.

Makes 2 dozen cookies

CHOCOLATE MACADAMIA CHIPPERS

Peanut Butter, Oatmeal, Cherry and Chip Mini Cookies

½ **cup granulated sugar**
⅓ **cup butter, softened**
¼ **cup packed brown sugar**
¼ **cup creamy peanut butter**
¼ **cup cholesterol-free egg substitute**
½ **teaspoon vanilla**
 1 **cup uncooked quick-cooking oats**
⅓ **cup all-purpose flour**
¼ **cup whole wheat flour**
½ **teaspoon baking powder**
¼ **teaspoon baking soda**
⅓ **cup mini semisweet chocolate chips**
¼ **cup dried cherries, coarsely chopped**

1. Preheat oven to 375°F.

2. Combine granulated sugar, butter, brown sugar and peanut butter in large bowl. Beat with electric mixer at medium speed until creamy. Add egg substitute and vanilla; beat until well blended. Add oats, flours, baking powder and baking soda. Beat at low speed until blended. Stir in chocolate chips and cherries.

3. Drop mixture by slightly rounded teaspoonfuls onto ungreased cookie sheets. Bake 8 to 9 minutes or until light brown. Cool on cookie sheets 1 minute. Transfer to wire racks; cool completely.   *Makes 96 mini cookies*

Prep Time: 10 minutes
Bake Time: 8 minutes

PEANUT BUTTER, OATMEAL, CHERRY AND CHIP MINI COOKIES

JUMBO 3-CHIP COOKIES

4 cups all-purpose flour
1 teaspoon baking powder
1 teaspoon baking soda
1½ cups (3 sticks) butter, softened
1¼ cups granulated sugar
1¼ cups packed brown sugar
2 large eggs
1 tablespoon vanilla extract
1 cup (6 ounces) NESTLÉ® TOLL HOUSE® Milk Chocolate Morsels
1 cup (6 ounces) NESTLÉ® TOLL HOUSE® Semi-Sweet Chocolate Morsels
½ cup NESTLÉ® TOLL HOUSE® Premier White Morsels
1 cup chopped nuts

PREHEAT oven to 375°F.

COMBINE flour, baking powder and baking soda in medium bowl. Beat butter, granulated sugar and brown sugar in large mixer bowl until creamy. Beat in eggs and vanilla extract. Gradually beat in flour mixture. Stir in morsels and nuts. Drop dough by level ¼-cup measure 2 inches apart onto ungreased baking sheets.

BAKE for 12 to 14 minutes or until light golden brown. Cool on baking sheets for 2 minutes; remove to wire racks to cool completely.

Makes about 2 dozen cookies

JUMBO 3-CHIP COOKIES

CHEWY OATMEAL TRAIL MIX COOKIES

¾ CRISCO® Butter Flavor Stick or ¾ cup CRISCO® Butter Flavor Shortening
  plus additional for greasing
1¼ cups firmly packed light brown sugar
  1 egg
⅓ cup milk
1½ teaspoons vanilla
2½ cups quick oats, uncooked
  1 cup PILLSBURY BEST® All-Purpose Flour
½ teaspoon baking soda
½ teaspoon salt
¼ teaspoon ground cinnamon
  1 cup (6 ounces) semisweet or milk chocolate chips
¾ cup raisins
¾ cup coarsely chopped walnuts, pecans or peanuts
½ cup sunflower seeds, shelled

1. Heat oven to 375°F. Grease baking sheets. Place sheets of foil on countertop for cooling cookies.

2. Combine ¾ stick CRISCO Shortening, brown sugar, egg, milk and vanilla in large bowl. Beat at medium speed of electric mixer until well blended.

3. Combine oats, flour, baking soda, salt and cinnamon. Mix into CRISCO Shortening mixture at low speed just until blended. Stir in chocolate chips, raisins, nuts and sunflower seeds.

4. Drop rounded tablespoonfuls of dough 2 inches apart onto prepared baking sheets.

5. Bake one baking sheet at a time at 375°F for 10 to 12 minutes or until lightly browned. *Do not overbake.* Cool 2 minutes on baking sheets. Remove cookies to foil to cool completely.   *Makes about 3 dozen cookies*

Note: You may substitute 3 cups of prepared trail mix (available in grocery or health food stores) for the chips, raisins, nuts and sunflower seeds.

CHEWY OATMEAL TRAIL MIX COOKIES

HONEY CHOCOLATE CHIPPERS

- 1 cup honey
- 1 cup (2 sticks) butter or margarine, softened
- 1 egg yolk
- 1 teaspoon vanilla extract
- 2 cups all-purpose flour
- 1 cup rolled oats
- ½ teaspoon baking soda
- ½ teaspoon salt
- 1 cup chopped toasted pecans
- 1 cup (6 ounces) semi-sweet chocolate chips

In medium bowl, beat honey and butter until creamy but not fluffy. Beat in egg yolk and vanilla. In separate bowl, combine flour, oats, baking soda and salt. Stir dry ingredients into wet mixture until thoroughly blended. Mix in pecans and chocolate chips. Chill dough for 30 minutes. Drop dough by rounded tablespoons onto ungreased cookie sheets. Flatten each cookie with a spoon. Bake at 350°F for 15 to 20 minutes, or until tops are dry. Cool on wire racks.

Makes 2 dozen cookies

Favorite recipe from **National Honey Board**

Baking Tips

Space the mounds of dough about 2 inches apart on cookie sheets to allow for spreading unless the recipe directs otherwise.

CRUNCHY & CHIPPY PEANUT BUTTER COOKIES

1¼ cups firmly packed light brown sugar
¾ cup JIF® Crunchy Peanut Butter
½ CRISCO® Stick or ½ cup CRISCO® Shortening
3 tablespoons milk
1 tablespoon vanilla
1 egg
1¾ cups PILLSBURY BEST® All-Purpose Flour
¾ teaspoon baking soda
¾ teaspoon salt
1 cup (6 ounces) miniature semisweet chocolate chips
1 cup chopped peanuts*

Salted, unsalted or dry roasted peanuts can be used.

1. Heat oven to 375°F. Place sheets of foil on countertop for cooling cookies.

2. Place brown sugar, peanut butter, CRISCO Shortening, milk and vanilla in large bowl. Beat at medium speed of electric mixer until well blended. Add egg; beat just until blended.

3. Combine flour, baking soda and salt. Add to CRISCO Shortening mixture; beat at low speed just until blended. Stir in miniature chocolate chips and peanuts.

4. Drop dough by rounded measuring tablespoonfuls 2 inches apart onto ungreased baking sheets. Flatten slightly with fingers.

5. Bake one baking sheet at a time at 375°F for 7 to 8 minutes or until cookies are set and just beginning to brown. *Do not overbake.* Cool 2 minutes on baking sheet. Remove cookies to foil to cool completely.

Makes about 3 dozen cookies

CHERRY CHOCOLATE CHIP WALNUT COOKIES

- 1 cup sugar
- ¼ cup Dried Plum Purée (recipe follows) or prepared dried plum butter *or*
     1 jar (2½ ounces) first-stage baby food dried plums
- ¼ cup water
- 2 tablespoons nonfat milk
- 1 teaspoon vanilla
- ½ teaspoon instant espresso coffee powder *or* 1 teaspoon instant coffee
     granules
- 1 cup all-purpose flour
- ½ cup unsweetened cocoa powder
- ¾ teaspoon baking soda
- ½ teaspoon salt
- ½ cup dried sour cherries
- ¼ cup chopped walnuts
- ¼ cup semisweet chocolate chips

Preheat oven to 350°F. Coat baking sheets with vegetable cooking spray. In large bowl, whisk together sugar, Dried Plum Purée, water, milk, vanilla and espresso powder until mixture is well blended, about 1 minute. Combine flour, cocoa, baking soda and salt; mix into dried plum purée mixture until well blended. Stir in cherries, walnuts and chocolate chips. Spoon twelve equal mounds of dough onto prepared baking sheets, spacing at least 2 inches apart. Bake in center of oven 18 to 20 minutes or until set and tops of cookies feel dry to the touch. Cool on baking sheets 2 minutes; remove to wire rack to cool completely.   *Makes 12 large cookies*

Plum Purée: Combine 1⅓ cups (8 ounces) pitted dried plums and 6 tablespoons hot water in container of food processor or blender. Pulse on and off until dried plums are finely chopped and smooth. Store leftovers in covered container in refrigerator for up to two months. Makes 1 cup purée.

*Favorite recipe from **California Dried Plum Board***

CHERRY CHOCOLATE CHIP WALNUT COOKIES

PASTEL MINT SWIRLS

⅓ cup coarse or granulated sugar
1 package (18¼ ounces) devil's food cake mix *without* pudding in the mix
3 eggs
¼ cup (½ stick) butter, melted
¼ cup unsweetened cocoa powder
144 small or 48 large pastel mint chips

1. Preheat oven to 375°F. Place sugar in shallow bowl.

2. Combine cake mix, eggs, butter and cocoa in large bowl just until blended. (Dough will be stiff.)

3. Shape dough into 1-inch balls; roll in sugar to coat. Place 2 inches apart on ungreased cookie sheets.

4. Bake 8 to 9 minutes or until tops are cracked. Gently press 3 small or 1 large mint into top of each cookie. Cool on cookie sheet 1 minute; transfer to wire racks to cool completely.   *Makes 48 cookies*

Baking Tips

Cookies that are uniform in size and shape will finish baking at the same time. To easily shape drop cookies into a uniform size, use an ice cream scoop with a release bar. The bar usually has a number on it indicating the number of scoops that can be made from one quart of ice cream. The handiest size for cookies is a #40, #50 or #80 scoop.

PASTEL MINT SWIRLS

FRUIT AND NUT CHIPPERS

            1 cup (2 sticks) butter, softened
            ¾ cup granulated sugar
            ¾ cup packed light brown sugar
            2 eggs
            1 teaspoon vanilla
        2¼ cups all-purpose flour
            1 teaspoon baking soda
            ½ teaspoon salt
            1 package (11½ ounces) milk chocolate chips
            1 cup chopped dried apricots
            1 cup chopped pecans or walnuts

1. Preheat oven to 375°F.

2. Combine butter and sugars in large bowl. Beat with electric mixer at medium speed until light and fluffy. Beat in eggs and vanilla. Combine flour, baking soda and salt in medium bowl; add to butter mixture. Beat until well blended. Stir in chocolate chips, apricots and pecans.

3. Drop dough by heaping teaspoonfuls 2 inches apart onto cookie sheets. Bake 9 to 10 minutes or until edges are golden brown. Cool on cookie sheets 2 minutes. Remove cookies to wire racks; cool completely.

Makes about 5 dozen cookies

FRUIT AND NUT CHIPPERS

REESE'S® PEANUT BUTTER AND MILK CHOCOLATE CHIP TASSIES

¾ cup (1½ sticks) butter, softened
1 package (3 ounces) cream cheese, softened
1½ cups all-purpose flour
¾ cup sugar, divided
1 egg, lightly beaten
2 tablespoons butter or margarine, melted
¼ teaspoon lemon juice
¼ teaspoon vanilla extract
1¾ cups (11-ounce package) REESE'S® Peanut Butter and Milk Chocolate Chips, divided
2 teaspoons shortening (do not use butter, margarine, spread or oil)

1. Beat ¾ cup butter and cream cheese with electric mixer on medium speed in medium bowl until well blended; add flour and ¼ cup sugar, beating until well blended. Cover; refrigerate about 1 hour or until dough is firm. Shape dough into 1-inch balls; press balls onto bottoms and up sides of 36 small muffin cups (1¾ inches in diameter).

2. Heat oven to 350°F. Combine egg, remaining ½ cup sugar, melted butter, lemon juice and vanilla in small bowl; stir until smooth. Set aside ⅓ cup chips; add remainder to egg mixture. Evenly fill muffin cups with chip mixture.

3. Bake 20 to 25 minutes or until filling is set and lightly browned. Cool completely; remove from pan to wire rack.

4. Combine reserved ⅓ cup chips and shortening in small microwave-safe bowl. Microwave at HIGH (100%) 30 seconds; stir. If necessary, microwave additional 15 seconds at a time, stirring after each heating, until chips are melted and mixture is smooth when stirred. Drizzle over tops of tassies.

Makes 3 dozen cookies

REESE'S® PEANUT BUTTER AND MILK CHOCOLATE CHIP TASSIES

GARBAGE PAIL COOKIES

   1 package (18¼ ounces) white cake mix with pudding in the mix
   ½ cup (1 stick) butter, softened
   2 eggs
   1 teaspoon vanilla
   1 teaspoon ground cinnamon
   ½ cup mini candy-coated chocolate pieces
   ½ cup salted peanuts
   ½ cup peanut butter chips
1½ cups crushed salted potato chips

1. Preheat oven to 350°F. Lightly grease cookie sheets.

2. Combine half of cake mix, butter, eggs, vanilla and cinnamon in large bowl. Beat with electric mixer at medium speed until light and fluffy. Beat in remaining cake mix until well blended. Stir in candy-coated chocolate pieces, peanuts and peanut butter chips. Stir in potato chips. (Dough will be stiff.)

3. Drop batter by rounded tablespoonfuls 2 inches apart onto prepared cookie sheets.

4. Bake 15 minutes or until golden brown. Cool on cookie sheets 2 minutes; transfer to wire racks to cool completely.   *Makes 40 cookies*

GARBAGE PAIL COOKIES

CHUNKY CHOCOLATE CHIP PEANUT BUTTER COOKIES

1¼ cups all-purpose flour
½ teaspoon baking soda
½ teaspoon salt
½ teaspoon ground cinnamon
¾ cup (1½ sticks) butter or margarine, softened
½ cup packed granulated sugar
½ cup brown sugar
½ cup creamy peanut butter
1 large egg
1 teaspoon vanilla extract
2 cups (12-ounce package) **NESTLÉ® TOLL HOUSE®** Semi-Sweet Chocolate Morsels
½ cup coarsely chopped peanuts

PREHEAT oven to 375°F.

COMBINE flour, baking soda, salt and cinnamon in small bowl. Beat butter, granulated sugar, brown sugar and peanut butter in large mixer bowl until creamy. Beat in egg and vanilla extract. Gradually beat in flour mixture. Stir in morsels and peanuts.

DROP dough by rounded tablespoon onto ungreased baking sheets. Press down slightly to flatten into 2-inch circles.

BAKE for 7 to 10 minutes or until edges are set but centers are still soft. Cool on baking sheets for 4 minutes; remove to wire racks to cool completely.

Makes about 3 dozen cookies

CHUNKY CHOCOLATE CHIP PEANUT BUTTER COOKIES

For Santa's Plate

MILK CHOCOLATE FLORENTINE COOKIES

⅔ cup butter

2 cups quick oats

1 cup granulated sugar

⅔ cup all-purpose flour

¼ cup light or dark corn syrup

¼ cup milk

1 teaspoon vanilla extract

¼ teaspoon salt

1¾ cups (11.5-ounce package) NESTLÉ® TOLL HOUSE® Milk Chocolate Morsels

PREHEAT oven to 375°F. Line baking sheets with foil.

MELT butter in medium saucepan; remove from heat. Stir in oats, sugar, flour, corn syrup, milk, vanilla extract and salt; mix well. Drop by level teaspoon, about 3 inches apart, onto prepared baking sheets. Spread thinly with rubber spatula.

BAKE for 6 to 8 minutes or until golden brown. Cool completely on baking sheets on wire racks. Peel foil from cookies.

MICROWAVE morsels in medium, uncovered, microwave-safe bowl on MEDIUM-HIGH (70%) power for 1 minute. Stir. Morsels may retain some of their original shape. If necessary, microwave at additional 10- to 15-second intervals, stirring just until morsels are melted. Spread thin layer of melted chocolate onto flat side of *half* the cookies. Top with *remaining* cookies.

Makes about 3½ dozen sandwich cookies

MILK CHOCOLATE FLORENTINE COOKIES

CHOCOLATE GINGERBREAD COOKIES

½ cup (1 stick) unsalted butter, softened
½ cup packed light brown sugar
¼ cup granulated sugar
1 tablespoon shortening
4 ounces semisweet chocolate, melted and cooled
2 tablespoons molasses
1 egg
2¼ cups all-purpose flour
3 tablespoons unsweetened cocoa powder
2½ teaspoons ground ginger
½ teaspoon baking soda
½ teaspoon ground cinnamon
⅛ teaspoon salt
⅛ teaspoon finely ground black pepper
Prepared icing (optional)

1. Combine butter, sugars and shortening in large bowl. Beat with electric mixer at medium speed until creamy. Add chocolate; beat until blended. Add molasses and egg; beat until well blended. Combine flour, cocoa, ginger, baking soda, cinnamon, salt and pepper in medium bowl. Gradually add flour mixture to butter mixture, beating until well blended. Divide dough in half. Wrap each half in plastic wrap; refrigerate at least 1 hour.

2. Preheat oven to 350°F. Roll out half of dough between sheets of plastic wrap to about ¼-inch thickness. Cut out shapes with 5-inch cookie cutters; place cutouts on ungreased cookie sheets. Refrigerate at least 15 minutes. Repeat with remaining dough.

3. Bake 8 to 10 minutes or until cookies have puffed slightly and have small crackles on surfaces. Cool 5 minutes on cookie sheets; remove to wire racks to cool completely. Decorate cooled cookies with icing, if desired.

Makes about 2 dozen 5-inch cookies

Chewy Chocolate Gingerbread Drops: Decrease flour to 1¾ cups. Shape 1½ teaspoonfuls of dough into balls. Place on ungreased cookie sheets. Flatten balls slightly and do not refrigerate before baking. Bake as directed above. Makes about 4½ dozen cookies.

CHOCOLATE GINGERBREAD COOKIES

EGGNOG COOKIES

Cookies
 1 cup (2 sticks) unsalted butter, softened
 1¼ cups plus 1 tablespoon granulated sugar, divided
 1 egg yolk
 ½ cup sour cream
 2½ cups all-purpose flour
 ¼ teaspoon salt
 ½ teaspoon grated nutmeg
 ¼ teaspoon ground ginger

Filling
 ½ cup (1 stick) unsalted butter, softened
 ¼ cup shortening
 2½ cups powdered sugar
 2 tablespoons brandy, Armagnac or milk

1. Preheat oven to 350°F. Lightly grease cookie sheets.

2. For cookies, combine butter and 1¼ cups granulated sugar in large bowl. Beat with electric mixer at medium speed until light and fluffy. Add egg yolk; beat until blended. Add sour cream; beat until well blended. Combine flour and salt in medium bowl. Gradually add flour mixture to butter mixture, beating until well blended.

3. Shape dough by rounded teaspoons balls. Place on prepared cookie sheets; flatten slightly. Combine remaining 1 tablespoon granulated sugar, nutmeg and ginger in small bowl; sprinkle over cookies.

4. Bake about 12 minutes or until edges are light brown. Cool 5 minutes on cookie sheets. Remove to wire racks to cool completely.

5. For filling, combine butter and shortening in medium bowl. Beat with electric mixer at medium speed until well blended. Add powdered sugar and brandy; beat until well blended. Spread or pipe filling on bottoms of half the cooled cookies. Top with remaining cookies.

Makes about 6 dozen cookies

EGGNOG COOKIES

HOLIDAY SUGAR COOKIES

> 1 cup (2 sticks) butter, softened
> ¾ cup sugar
> 1 egg
> 2 cups all-purpose flour
> 1 teaspoon baking powder
> ¼ teaspoon salt
> ¼ teaspoon ground cinnamon
>   Colored sprinkles or sugars (optional)

1. Combine butter and sugar in large bowl. Beat with electric mixer at medium speed until creamy. Add egg; beat until fluffy.

2. Stir in flour, baking powder, salt and cinnamon until well blended. Form dough into ball; wrap in plastic wrap and flatten. Refrigerate about 2 hours or until firm.

3. Preheat oven to 350°F. Roll out dough, small portions at a time, to ¼-inch thickness on lightly floured surface with lightly floured rolling pin. (Keep remaining dough wrapped in refrigerator.)

4. Cut out dough with 3-inch cookie cutters. Sprinkle with colored sprinkles or sugars, if desired. Transfer to ungreased cookie sheets.

5. Bake 7 to 9 minutes until edges are lightly browned. Cool on cookie sheets 1 minute; transfer to wire racks to cool completely. Store in airtight container.

Makes about 3 dozen cookies

HOLIDAY SUGAR COOKIES

Kentucky Bourbon Pecan Drops

Cookies

> 1 cup (2 sticks) butter, softened
> ¾ cup granulated sugar
> ¾ cup packed light brown sugar
> 2 eggs
> 1 tablespoon bourbon
> 2¼ cups all-purpose flour
> 1 teaspoon baking soda
> ½ teaspoon salt
> 1 cup coarsely chopped pecans, toasted

Chocolate-Bourbon Drizzle

> 1 cup semisweet chocolate chips
> 1 tablespoon butter
> 2 tablespoons heavy cream or half-and-half
> ½ cup sifted powdered sugar
> 3 tablespoons bourbon

1. Preheat oven to 350°F. For cookies, combine butter and sugars in large bowl. Beat with electric mixer at medium speed until light and fluffy. Beat in eggs and bourbon.

2. Combine flour, baking soda and salt. Gradually add to butter mixture, beating at low speed until dough forms. Beat in pecans.

3. Drop heaping tablespoonfuls of dough 2 inches apart on ungreased cookie sheets. Bake 12 to 14 minutes or until set and edges are golden brown. Cool on cookie sheets 1 minute. Remove cookies to wire racks; cool completely.

4. For drizzle, combine chocolate chips and butter in medium microwavable bowl. Microwave on HIGH 50 seconds; stir well. If necessary, microwave at 10 second intervals until chocolate is completely melted when stirred. Stir cream into chocolate, then powdered sugar; mix well. Stir in bourbon until well blended. Let stand at room temperature until completely cooled.

5. Transfer chocolate mixture to small plastic food storage bag. Cut very tiny corner off bag; drizzle decoratively over cookies. Let stand until chocolate is set.

6. Store tightly covered at room temperature or freeze cookies up to 3 months.   *Makes about 2½ dozen cookies*

NO-BAKE CHERRY CRISPS

¼ cup (½ stick) butter, softened
1 cup powdered sugar
1 cup peanut butter
1⅓ cups crisp rice cereal
½ cup maraschino cherries, drained, dried and chopped
¼ cup plus 2 tablespoons mini semisweet chocolate chips
¼ cup chopped pecans
1 to 2 cups flaked coconut

1. Beat butter, powdered sugar and peanut butter in large bowl. Stir in cereal, cherries, chocolate chips and pecans. Mix well.

2. Shape teaspoonfuls of mixture into 1-inch balls. Roll in coconut. Place on cookie sheets and refrigerate 1 hour. Store in refrigerator.
                                        Makes about 3 dozen cookies

MINT CHOCOLATE DELIGHTS

Cookies
- ½ cup (1 stick) unsalted butter, softened
- ½ cup granulated sugar
- ⅓ cup packed light brown sugar
- ⅓ cup semisweet chocolate chips, melted
- 1 egg, beaten
- ½ teaspoon vanilla
- 1½ cups all-purpose flour
- ¼ cup unsweetened cocoa powder
- ¼ teaspoon salt

Mint Filling
- 2½ cups powdered sugar
- ½ cup (1 stick) unsalted butter, softened
- ¼ teaspoon salt
- ½ teaspoon mint extract
- 3 to 4 drops red food coloring
- 2 to 3 tablespoons milk or half-and-half

1. For cookies, combine butter and sugars in large bowl. Beat with electric mixer at medium speed until creamy. Add melted chocolate, egg and vanilla; beat until well blended, scraping down bowl occasionally. Combine flour, cocoa and salt in small bowl. Gradually add flour mixture, beating until well blended. Shape dough into 16-inch-long log. Wrap in plastic wrap; refrigerate about 1 hour or until firm.

2. Preheat oven to 400°F. Lightly grease cookie sheets and line with parchment paper. Cut log into ⅓-inch-thick slices. Place slices on prepared cookie sheets. Bake 10 to 12 minutes or until set. Cool 5 minutes on cookie sheets. Remove to wire racks to cool completely.

3. For filling, combine powdered sugar, butter and salt in large bowl; beat until well blended. Add mint extract and food coloring; beat until well blended and evenly tinted. Add enough milk, 1 tablespoon at a time, to make filling fluffy. Spread or pipe filling on bottoms of half of cookies. Top with remaining cookies. *Makes 24 sandwich cookies*

MINT CHOCOLATE DELIGHTS

GINGER SHORTBREAD DELIGHTS

 1 cup (2 sticks) unsalted butter, softened
 ½ cup powdered sugar
 ⅓ cup packed light brown sugar
 ½ teaspoon salt
 2 cups minus 2 tablespoons all-purpose flour
 4 ounces crystallized ginger
   Bittersweet Glaze (recipe follows)

1. Preheat oven to 300°F.

2. Combine butter, sugars and salt in large bowl. Beat with electric mixer at medium speed until creamy. Gradually add flour, beating until well blended.

3. Shape dough by tablespoons into balls. Place 1 inch apart on ungreased cookie sheets; flatten to ½-inch thickness. Cut ginger into ¼-inch-thick slices. Place 1 slice ginger on top of each cookie.

4. Bake 20 minutes or until set and lightly browned. Cool 5 minutes on cookie sheets. Remove to wire racks to cool completely.

5. Prepare Bittersweet Glaze; drizzle over cookies. Let stand about 30 minutes or until glaze is set. *Makes about 3½ dozen cookies*

BITTERSWEET GLAZE

 1 bar (about 3 ounces) bittersweet chocolate, broken into small pieces
 2 tablespoons unsalted butter
 2 tablespoons whipping cream
 1 tablespoon powdered sugar
 ⅛ teaspoon salt

Melt chocolate and butter in top of double boiler over hot, not boiling, water. Remove from heat. Add cream, powdered sugar and salt; stir until smooth.

GINGER SHORTBREAD DELIGHTS

CHRISTMAS WREATHS

1 package (18 ounces) refrigerated sugar cookie dough
2 tablespoons all-purpose flour
   Green food coloring
   Small red candies
   Green colored sugar or sprinkles
   Red decorating icing

1. Remove dough from wrapper; place in large bowl. Let dough stand at room temperature about 15 minutes.

2. Add flour and green food coloring to dough in bowl; beat at medium speed of electric mixer until dough is well blended and evenly colored. Divide dough in half; wrap both halves in plastic wrap and freeze 20 minutes.

3. Preheat oven to 350°F. Grease cookie sheets. For cookie bottoms, roll one half of dough on lightly floured surface to ⅜-inch thickness. Cut with 3-inch round or fluted cookie cutter; place 2 inches apart on prepared cookie sheets. Using 1-inch round cookie cutter, cut center circle from each cookie.

4. For cookie tops, roll remaining half of dough on lightly floured surface to ⅜-inch thickness. Cut with 3-inch round or fluted cookie cutter; place 2 inches apart on prepared cookie sheets. Using 1-inch round cookie cutter, cut center circle from each cookie. Using hors d'oeuvre cutters, miniature cookie cutters or knife, cut out tiny circles and insert red candies as shown in photo. Decorate with green sugar or sprinkles as desired.

5. Bake cutouts 10 minutes or until very lightly browned at edges. Cool on cookie sheet 5 minutes; remove to wire racks to cool completely.

6. To assemble, spread icing on flat sides of bottom cookies; place top cookies over icing.   *Makes about 1½ dozen sandwich cookies*

CHRISTMAS WREATHS

ORANGE-ALMOND SABLES

1½ cups powdered sugar
1 cup (2 sticks) butter, softened
1 tablespoon finely grated orange peel
1 tablespoon almond-flavored liqueur *or* 1 teaspoon almond extract
¾ cup whole blanched almonds, toasted*
1¾ cups all-purpose flour
¼ teaspoon salt
1 egg, beaten

To toast almonds, spread in single layer on baking sheet. Bake in preheated 350°F oven 8 to 10 minutes or until brown, stirring twice.

1. Preheat oven to 375°F.

2. Combine powdered sugar and butter in large bowl. Beat with electric mixer at medium speed until light and fluffy. Beat in orange peel and liqueur.

3. Reserve 24 whole almonds. Place remaining cooled almonds in food processor. Process using on/off pulses until almonds are ground, but not pasty.

4. Combine ground almonds, flour and salt in medium bowl; stir. Gradually add to butter mixture. Beat with electric mixer at low speed until well blended.

5. Roll dough on lightly floured surface with lightly floured rolling pin to just under ¼-inch thickness. Cut dough with floured 2½-inch fluted or round cookie cutter. Place cutouts 2 inches apart on ungreased cookie sheets.

6. Lightly brush tops of cutouts with beaten egg. Press one whole reserved almond in center of each cutout. Brush almond lightly with beaten egg. Bake 10 to 12 minutes or until light golden brown.

7. Cool 1 minute on cookie sheets. Remove cookies to wire racks; cool completely. Store tightly covered at room temperature, or freeze up to 3 months.   *Makes about 2 dozen cookies*

CRISPY THUMBPRINT COOKIES

1 package (18¼ ounces) yellow cake mix
½ cup vegetable oil
¼ cup water
1 egg
3 cups crisp rice cereal, crushed
½ cup chopped walnuts
6 tablespoons raspberry or strawberry preserves

1. Preheat oven to 375°F.

2. Combine cake mix, oil, water and egg in large bowl. Beat with electric mixer at medium speed until well blended. Add cereal and walnuts; mix until well blended.

3. Drop by heaping teaspoonfuls about 2 inches apart onto ungreased cookie sheets. Use thumb to make indentation in each cookie. Spoon about ½ teaspoon preserves into center of each cookie.

4. Bake 9 to 11 minutes or until golden brown. Cool cookies 1 minute on cookie sheets. Remove to wire racks to cool completely.

Makes 3 dozen cookies

Prep Time: **20 minutes**
Bake Time: **9 to 11 minutes**

Rum Fruitcake Cookies

1 cup sugar
¾ cup shortening
3 eggs
⅓ cup orange juice
1 tablespoon rum extract
3 cups all-purpose flour
2 teaspoons baking powder
1 teaspoon baking soda
1 teaspoon salt
2 cups (8 ounces) chopped candied mixed fruit
1 cup raisins
1 cup nuts, coarsely chopped

1. Preheat oven to 375°F. Lightly grease cookie sheets; set aside.

2. Combine sugar and shortening in large bowl. Beat with electric mixer at medium speed until fluffy. Add eggs, orange juice and rum extract; beat 2 minutes.Combine flour, baking powder, baking soda and salt in medium bowl. Add candied fruit, raisins and nuts. Stir into shortening mixture. Drop dough by rounded teaspoonfuls 2 inches apart onto prepared cookie sheets.

3. Bake 10 to 12 minutes or until light brown. Cool cookies on cookie sheets 2 minutes. Remove to wire racks; cool completely.

Makes about 6 dozen cookies

RUM FRUITCAKE COOKIES

HOLIDAY DOUBLE PEANUT BUTTER FUDGE COOKIES

1 can (14 ounces) sweetened condensed milk (not evaporated milk)
¾ cup REESE'S® Creamy Peanut Butter
2 cups all-purpose biscuit baking mix
1 teaspoon vanilla extract
¾ cup REESE'S® Peanut Butter Chips
¼ cup granulated sugar
½ teaspoon red colored sugar
½ teaspoon green colored sugar

1. Heat oven to 375°F.

2. Beat sweetened condensed milk and peanut butter with electric mixer on medium speed in large bowl until smooth. Beat in baking mix and vanilla; stir in peanut butter chips. Set aside.

3. Stir together granulated sugar and colored sugars in small bowl. Shape dough into 1-inch balls; roll in sugar. Place 2 inches apart on ungreased cookie sheet; flatten slightly with bottom of glass.

4. Bake 6 to 8 minutes or until very lightly browned (do not overbake). Cool slightly. Remove to wire rack and cool completely. Store in tightly covered container.

Makes about 3½ dozen cookies

Baking Tips

To avoid overbaking cookies, check them at the minimum baking time. If more time is needed, watch them carefully to make sure they do not overbake. It is better to slightly underbake than overbake cookies.

HOLIDAY DOUBLE PEANUT BUTTER FUDGE COOKIES

PEPPERMINT COOKIES

    1 cup firmly packed light brown sugar
    ¾ CRISCO® Butter Flavor Stick or ¾ cup CRISCO® Butter Flavor Shortening
    2 tablespoons milk
    1 tablespoon vanilla
    1 egg
    1¾ cups PILLSBURY BEST® All-Purpose Flour
    1 teaspoon salt
    ¾ teaspoon baking soda
    ⅔ cup crushed peppermint candy canes*

To crush candy canes, break into small pieces. Place in plastic food storage bag. Secure top. Use rolling pin to break candy into very small pieces.

1. Heat oven to 375°F. Place sheets of foil on countertop for cooling cookies.

2. Combine brown sugar, CRISCO Shortening, milk and vanilla in large bowl. Beat at medium speed of electric mixer until well blended. Beat egg into creamed mixture.

3. Combine flour, salt and baking soda. Mix into creamed mixture at low speed just until blended. Stir in crushed candy.

4. Shape dough into 1-inch balls. Place 2 inches apart on ungreased baking sheet.

5. Bake 1 baking sheet at a time at 375°F for 8 to 10 minutes for chewy cookies or 11 to 13 minutes for crisp cookies. *Do not overbake.* Cool 2 minutes on baking sheet. Remove cookies to foil to cool completely.

Makes about 3 dozen cookies

PEPPERMINT COOKIES

MOLASSES SPICE COOKIES

    1 cup granulated sugar
    ¾ cup shortening
    ¼ cup molasses
    1 egg, beaten
    2 cups all-purpose flour
    2 teaspoons baking soda
    1 teaspoon ground ginger
    1 teaspoon ground cinnamon
    1 teaspoon ground cloves
    ¼ teaspoon salt
    ¼ teaspoon dry mustard
    ½ cup granulated brown sugar or granulated sugar

1. Preheat oven to 375°F. Grease cookie sheets; set aside.

2. Combine granulated sugar and shortening in large bowl. Beat with electric mixer at medium speed about 5 minutes until light and fluffy. Add molasses and egg; beat until fluffy.

3. Combine flour, baking soda, ginger, cinnamon, cloves, salt and mustard in medium bowl. Add to shortening mixture; beat until just blended.

4. Place brown sugar in shallow dish. Shape dough into 1-inch balls; roll in sugar to coat. Place 2 inches apart on prepared cookie sheets. Bake 15 minutes or until lightly browned. Cool cookies on cookie sheets 2 minutes. Remove cookies to wire racks; cool completely.

Makes about 6 dozen cookies

Helpful Hint: Looking for something different to take to all your holiday gatherings? Decorate a metal tin with rubber stamps for a crafty look and fill it with Molasses Spice Cookies and an assortment of uniquely flavored teas. Perfect for a twist on your traditional hostess gift.

DOUBLE CHOCOLATE SANDWICH COOKIES

1 package (18 ounces) refrigerated sugar cookie dough
1 bar (3½ to 4 ounces) bittersweet chocolate, chopped
2 teaspoons butter
¾ cup milk chocolate chips

1. Preheat oven to 350°F. Remove dough from wrapper, keeping in log shape.

2. Cut dough into ¼-inch-thick slices. Arrange slices 2 inches apart on ungreased cookie sheets. Cut centers out of half of cookies using ½-inch round cookie cutter.

3. Bake 10 to 12 minutes or until edges are lightly browned. Cool on cookie sheets 2 minutes. Remove to wire racks; cool completely.

4. Place bittersweet chocolate and butter in small heavy saucepan. Heat over low heat, stirring frequently, until chocolate is melted. Spread chocolate over flat sides of cookies without holes. Immediately top each with cutout cookie.

5. Place milk chocolate chips in resealable plastic food storage bag; seal bag. Microwave on MEDIUM (50%) 1½ minutes. Turn bag over; microwave 1 to 1½ minutes more or until melted. Knead bag until chocolate is smooth.

6. Cut tiny corner off bag; drizzle chocolate decoratively over sandwich cookies. Let stand until chocolate is set, about 30 minutes.

Makes 16 sandwich cookies

Holiday Cookies on a Stick

2¼ cups all-purpose flour
  1 teaspoon baking soda
  1 teaspoon salt
  1 cup (2 sticks) butter, softened
  ¾ cup granulated sugar
  ¾ cup packed brown sugar
  1 teaspoon vanilla extract
  2 large eggs
1¾ cups (10-ounce package) NESTLÉ® TOLL HOUSE® Holiday Shapes & Morsels, *divided*
 12 wooden craft sticks
  1 can (16 ounces) cream cheese frosting

PREHEAT oven to 350°F.

COMBINE flour, baking soda and salt in small bowl. Beat butter, granulated sugar, brown sugar and vanilla extract in large mixer bowl until creamy. Add eggs, one at a time, beating well after each addition. Gradually beat in flour mixture. *Stir in ¾ cup Shapes & Morsels (set aside remaining Shapes & Morsels).* Drop dough by level ⅓-cup measure 3 inches apart on ungreased baking sheets. Shape into mounds with floured fingers; press down slightly. Insert wooden stick into side of each mound.

BAKE for 14 to 18 minutes or until golden brown. Cool on baking sheets on wire racks for 3 minutes; remove to wire racks to cool completely.

SPREAD frosting on tops of cookies. *Sprinkle with remaining Shapes & Morsels.*   *Makes about 12 large cookies*

HOLIDAY COOKIES ON A STICK

MINCEMEAT OATMEAL COOKIES

½ **CRISCO® Butter Flavor Stick or** ½ **cup CRISCO® Butter Flavor Shortening
plus additional for greasing**
1 **cup firmly packed brown sugar**
1 **egg**
1⅓ **cups prepared mincemeat**
1½ **cups PILLSBURY BEST® All-Purpose Flour**
1 **teaspoon baking soda**
½ **teaspoon salt**
1 **cup quick oats (not instant or old-fashioned)**
½ **cup coarsely chopped walnuts**

1. Heat oven to 350°F. Grease baking sheet with CRISCO Shortening. Place sheets of foil on countertop for cooling cookies.

2. Combine ½ stick CRISCO Shortening, sugar and egg in large bowl. Beat at medium speed of electric mixer until well blended. Beat in mincemeat.

3. Combine flour, baking soda and salt. Mix into creamed mixture at low speed until blended. Stir in oats and nuts with spoon.

4. Drop rounded tablespoonfuls of dough 2 inches apart onto prepared baking sheet.

5. Bake at 350°F for 12 minutes or until set and lightly browned around edges. *Do not overbake.* Cool 2 minutes on baking sheet. Remove cookies to foil to cool completely. *Makes about 5 dozen cookies*

CONTENTS

Beloved Brownies

Fudgy Hazelnut Brownies

1 (21-ounce) package DUNCAN HINES® Chewy Fudge Brownie Mix
2 eggs
½ cup vegetable oil
¼ cup water
1 cup chopped toasted hazelnuts
1 cup semisweet chocolate chips
1 cup DUNCAN HINES® Dark Chocolate Frosting
3 squares white chocolate, melted

1. Preheat oven to 350°F. Grease bottom only of 13×9-inch baking pan.

2. Combine brownie mix, eggs, oil and water in large bowl. Stir with spoon until well blended, about 50 strokes. Stir in hazelnuts and chocolate chips. Spread in prepared pan. Bake at 350°F for 25 to 30 minutes or until set. Cool completely.

3. Heat frosting in microwave oven at HIGH for 15 seconds or until thin; stir well. Spread over brownies. Spoon dollops of white chocolate over chocolate frosting; marble white chocolate through frosting. Cool completely. Cut into bars. *Makes 24 brownies*

FUDGY HAZELNUT BROWNIES

Five-Layer Brownie Dessert

1 package (19 to 21 ounces) chocolate brownie mix, plus ingredients to prepare mix

1 package (4-serving size) chocolate-flavored instant pudding mix, plus ingredients to prepare mix

4 to 5 cups powdered sugar

1 package (8 ounces) cream cheese, softened

2 cups (12 ounces) milk chocolate chips, divided

1 container (8 ounces) frozen whipped topping, thawed

1. Prepare brownie mix according to package directions for 13×9-inch pan. Set aside.

2. Prepare pudding mix according to package directions; set aside.

3. Combine powdered sugar and cream cheese in medium bowl. Beat with electric mixer at medium speed 1 minute. Set aside.

4. Sprinkle prepared brownies with 1½ cups chocolate chips. Evenly spread cream cheese mixture over chocolate chips. Spread pudding mixture over cream cheese mixture. Spread whipped topping over pudding mixture. Sprinkle remaining ½ cup chocolate chips over whipped topping. Refrigerate until ready to serve. *Makes 12 to 14 brownies*

FIVE-LAYER BROWNIE DESSERT

ALMOND BROWNIES

½ cup (1 stick) butter
2 squares (1 ounce each) unsweetened baking chocolate
2 large eggs
1 cup firmly packed light brown sugar
¼ teaspoon almond extract
½ cup all-purpose flour
1½ cups "M&M's"® Chocolate Mini Baking Bits, divided
½ cup slivered almonds, toasted and divided
Chocolate Glaze (recipe follows)

Preheat oven to 350°F. Grease and flour 8×8×2-inch baking pan; set aside. In small saucepan melt butter and chocolate over low heat; stir to blend. Remove from heat; let cool. In medium bowl beat eggs and brown sugar until well blended; stir in chocolate mixture and almond extract. Add flour. Stir in 1 cup "M&M's"® Chocolate Mini Baking Bits and ¼ cup almonds. Spread batter evenly in prepared pan. Bake 25 to 28 minutes or until firm in center. Cool completely on wire rack. Prepare Chocolate Glaze. Spread over brownies; decorate with remaining ½ cup "M&M's"® Chocolate Mini Baking Bits and remaining ¼ cup almonds. Cut into bars. Store in tightly covered container. *Makes 16 brownies*

Chocolate Glaze: In small saucepan over low heat combine 4 teaspoons water and 1 tablespoon butter until it comes to a boil. Stir in 4 teaspoons unsweetened cocoa powder. Gradually stir in ½ cup powdered sugar until smooth. Remove from heat; stir in ¼ teaspoon vanilla extract. Let glaze cool slightly.

ALMOND BROWNIES

CHEESECAKE-TOPPED BROWNIES

- 1 (19.5- or 19.8-ounce family-size) package fudge brownie mix, plus ingredients to prepare mix
- 1 (8-ounce) package cream cheese, softened
- 2 tablespoons butter or margarine, softened
- 1 tablespoon cornstarch
- 1 (14-ounce) can EAGLE BRAND® Sweetened Condensed Milk (NOT evaporated milk)
- 1 egg
- 2 teaspoons vanilla extract
- Ready-to-spread chocolate frosting (optional)
- Orange peel (optional)

1. Preheat oven to 350°F. Prepare brownie mix as package directs. Spread into well-greased 13×9-inch baking pan.

2. In large bowl, beat cream cheese, butter and cornstarch until fluffy.

3. Gradually beat in EAGLE BRAND®. Add egg and vanilla; beat until smooth. Pour cheesecake mixture evenly over brownie batter.

4. Bake 40 to 45 minutes or until top is lightly browned. Cool. Spread with frosting or sprinkle with orange peel (optional). Cut into bars. Store leftovers covered in refrigerator.

Makes 3 to 3½ dozen brownies

Prep Time: 20 minutes
Bake Time: 40 to 45 minutes

CHEESECAKE-TOPPED BROWNIES

Easy Double Chocolate Chip Brownies

2 cups (12-ounce package) NESTLÉ® TOLL HOUSE® Semi-Sweet Chocolate Morsels, *divided*
½ **cup (1 stick) butter or margarine, cut into pieces**
3 large eggs
1¼ **cups all-purpose flour**
1 cup granulated sugar
1 teaspoon vanilla extract
¼ **teaspoon baking soda**
½ **cup chopped nuts**

PREHEAT oven to 350°F. Grease 13×9-inch baking pan.

MELT *1 cup* morsels and butter in large, *heavy-duty* saucepan over low heat; stir until smooth. Remove from heat. Stir in eggs. Stir in flour, sugar, vanilla extract and baking soda. Stir in *remaining* morsels and nuts. Spread into prepared baking pan.

BAKE for 18 to 22 minutes or until wooden pick inserted in center comes out slightly sticky. Cool completely in pan on wire rack.

Makes 2 dozen brownies

Baking Tips

For easy removal of brownies and bar cookies (and no cleanup!), line the baking pan with foil and leave at least 3 inches hanging over each end. Use the foil to lift out the treats, place them on a cutting board and carefully remove the foil. Then simply cut them into pieces.

EASY DOUBLE CHOCOLATE CHIP BROWNIES

Coconut Crowned Cappuccino Brownies

- **6 squares (1 ounce each) semisweet chocolate, coarsely chopped**
- **1 tablespoon instant coffee granules**
- **1 tablespoon boiling water**
- **½ cup sugar**
- **¼ cup (½ stick) butter, softened**
- **3 eggs, divided**
- **¾ cup all-purpose flour**
- **¾ teaspoon ground cinnamon**
- **½ teaspoon baking powder**
- **¼ teaspoon salt**
- **¼ cup whipping cream**
- **1 teaspoon vanilla**
- **¾ cup flaked coconut, divided**
- **½ cup semisweet chocolate chips, divided**

1. Preheat oven to 350°F. Grease 8-inch square baking pan. Melt chocolate in small, heavy saucepan over low heat, stirring constantly; set aside. Dissolve coffee granules in boiling water in small cup; set aside. Combine sugar and butter in large bowl. Beat with electric mixer at medium speed until light and fluffy. Beat in 2 eggs, 1 at a time, scraping down side of bowl after each addition. Beat in chocolate and coffee mixture until well blended. Combine flour, cinnamon, baking powder and salt in small bowl; add to butter mixture. Beat until well blended. Spread evenly in prepared pan.

2. Combine whipping cream, remaining egg and vanilla in small bowl; blend well. Stir in ½ cup coconut and ¼ cup chocolate chips. Spread evenly over brownie batter; sprinkle with remaining ¼ cup coconut and ¼ cup chocolate chips. Bake 30 to 35 minutes or until coconut is browned and center is set. Remove pan to wire rack; cool completely. Cut into 2-inch squares.

Makes 16 brownies

PEANUT BUTTER MARBLED BROWNIES

4 ounces (half 8 ounce package) cream cheese, softened
½ cup peanut butter
2 tablespoons sugar
1 egg
1 package (19 to 21 ounces) brownie mix, plus ingredients to prepare mix
¾ cup lightly salted cocktail peanuts

1. Preheat oven to 350°F. Lightly grease 13×9-inch baking pan; set aside.

2. Combine cream cheese, peanut butter, sugar and egg in large bowl. Beat with electric mixer at medium speed until blended.

3. Prepare brownie mix according to package directions. Spread brownie batter evenly in prepared pan. Spoon peanut butter mixture in dollops over batter. Swirl peanut butter mixture into batter with tip of knife. Sprinkle peanuts on top; lightly press into batter.

4. Bake 30 to 35 minutes or until toothpick inserted into center comes out almost clean. Do not overbake. Cool brownies completely in pan on wire rack. Cut into squares. *Makes 2 dozen brownies*

DOUBLE MINT BROWNIES

1 (21-ounce) package DUNCAN HINES® Family-Style Chewy Fudge Brownie Mix
1 egg
⅓ cup water
⅓ cup vegetable oil plus additional for greasing
½ teaspoon peppermint extract
24 chocolate-covered peppermint patties (1½ inches each)
1 cup confectioners' sugar, divided
4 teaspoons milk, divided
Red food coloring
Green food coloring

1. Preheat oven to 350°F. Grease bottom only of 13×9×2-inch pan.

2. Combine brownie mix, egg, water, oil and peppermint extract in large bowl. Stir with spoon until well blended, about 50 strokes. Spread in prepared pan. Bake brownies following package directions. Place peppermint patties on warm brownies. Cool completely.

3. Combine ½ cup confectioners' sugar, 2 teaspoons milk and 1 drop red food coloring in small bowl. Stir until smooth. Place in small resealable plastic bag; set aside. Repeat with remaining ½ cup confectioners' sugar, remaining 2 teaspoons milk and 1 drop green food coloring. Cut pinpoint hole in bottom corner of each bag. Drizzle pink and green glazes over brownies. Allow glazes to set before cutting into bars.

Makes 24 brownies

Tip: To prevent overdone edges and underdone center, wrap foil strips around outside edges of pan (do not cover bottom or top). Bake as directed above.

DOUBLE MINT BROWNIES

Peanut Butter Fudge Brownie Bars

1 cup (2 sticks) butter or margarine, melted
1½ cups sugar
2 eggs
1 teaspoon vanilla extract
1¼ cups all-purpose flour
⅔ cup HERSHEY'S Cocoa
¼ cup milk
1¼ cups chopped pecans or walnuts, divided
½ cup (1 stick) butter or margarine
1⅔ cups (10-ounce package) REESE'S® Peanut Butter Chips
1 can (14 ounces) sweetened condensed milk (not evaporated milk)
¼ cup HERSHEY'S Semi-Sweet Chocolate Chips

1. Heat oven to 350°F. Grease 13×9×2-inch baking pan.

2. Beat melted butter, sugar, eggs and vanilla in large bowl with electric mixer on medium speed until well blended. Add flour, cocoa and milk; beat until blended. Stir in 1 cup nuts. Spread in prepared pan.

3. Bake 25 to 30 minutes or just until edges begin to pull away from sides of pan. Cool completely in pan on wire rack.

4. Melt ½ cup butter and peanut butter chips in medium saucepan over low heat, stirring constantly. Add sweetened condensed milk, stirring until smooth; pour over baked layer.

5. Place chocolate chips in small microwave-safe bowl. Microwave at HIGH (100%) 45 seconds or just until chips are melted when stirred. Drizzle bars with melted chocolate; sprinkle with remaining ¼ cup nuts. Refrigerate 1 hour or until firm. Cut into bars. Cover; refrigerate leftover bars.

Makes 36 bars

PEANUT BUTTER FUDGE BROWNIE BARS

CHUNKY CARAMEL NUT BROWNIES

- ¾ cup (1½ sticks) butter
- 4 squares (1 ounce each) unsweetened chocolate
- 2 cups sugar
- 4 eggs
- 1 cup all-purpose flour
- 1 package (14 ounces) caramels
- ¼ cup heavy cream
- 2 cups pecan halves or coarsely chopped pecans, divided
- 1 package (12 ounces) chocolate chunks or chips

1. Preheat oven to 350°F. Grease 13×9-inch baking pan; set aside.

2. Place butter and chocolate in large microwavable bowl. Microwave on HIGH 1½ to 2 minutes or until chocolate is melted and mixture is smooth when stirred. Stir in sugar until well blended. Beat in eggs with electric mixer at medium speed, one at a time. Stir in flour until well blended. Spread half of batter in prepared pan. Bake 20 minutes.

3. Meanwhile, combine caramels and cream in medium microwavable bowl. Microwave on HIGH 1½ to 2 minutes or until caramels begin to melt; stir until mixture is smooth. Stir in 1 cup pecan halves.

4. Spread caramel mixture over partially baked brownie base. Sprinkle with half of chocolate chunks. Pour remaining brownie batter over top; sprinkle with remaining 1 cup pecan halves and chocolate chunks. Bake 25 to 30 minutes or until set. Cool completely in pan on wire rack. Cut into squares.

Makes 2 dozen brownies

Chunky Caramel Nut Brownies

CHOCOLATE ESPRESSO BROWNIES

4 squares (1 ounce each) unsweetened chocolate
1 cup sugar
¼ cup Dried Plum Purée (recipe follows) or prepared dried plum butter
3 egg whites
1 to 2 tablespoons instant espresso coffee powder
1 teaspoon baking powder
1 teaspoon salt
1 teaspoon vanilla
½ cup all-purpose flour
　　Powdered sugar (optional)

Preheat oven to 350°F. Coat 8-inch square baking pan with vegetable cooking spray. In small heavy saucepan, melt chocolate over very low heat, stirring until melted and smooth. Remove from heat; cool. In mixer bowl, beat chocolate and remaining ingredients except flour and powdered sugar at medium speed until well blended; mix in flour. Spread batter evenly in prepared pan. Bake in center of oven about 30 minutes until pick inserted into center comes out clean. Cool completely in pan on wire rack. Dust with powdered sugar. Cut into 1⅓-inch squares.　　*Makes 36 brownies*

Dried Plum Purée: Combine 1⅓ cups (8 ounces) pitted dried plums and 6 tablespoons hot water in container of food processor or blender. Pulse on and off until dried plums are finely chopped and smooth. Store leftovers in a covered container in the refrigerator for up to two months. Makes 1 cup.

Favorite recipe from **California Dried Plum Board**

CHOCOLATE ESPRESSO BROWNIES

CHERRY CHEESE BROWNIES

1 (16-ounce) can dark sweet cherries
1 (15-ounce) brownie mix (8×8 pan size)
2 eggs, divided
¼ cup vegetable oil
1 (3-ounce) package cream cheese, softened
2 tablespoons granulated sugar
¾ cup flaked coconut
1 teaspoon almond extract

Drain cherries, reserving ¼ cup cherry juice. Place brownie mix in large bowl. Add 1 egg, oil and reserved cherry juice; mix well. Gently stir in cherries. Set aside.

Combine cream cheese and sugar in medium mixing bowl. Beat with electric mixer 3 to 4 minutes, or until well mixed. Add remaining egg; mix well. Stir in coconut and almond extract.

Lightly grease 8×8×2-inch baking pan. Spoon brownie mixture evenly into pan. Spoon cream cheese mixture over brownie mixture. Use knife to swirl cream cheese mixture into brownie mixture.

Bake in preheated 350°F oven 35 to 40 minutes, or until wooden pick inserted near center comes out clean. Let cool. Cut into squares or bars.

Makes 9 squares or 18 bars

Note: You can substitute ½ cup chopped pecans or walnuts for the coconut.

Favorite recipe from **Cherry Marketing Institute**

MOIST AND MINTY BROWNIES

Brownies
- 1¼ cups all-purpose flour
- ½ teaspoon baking soda
- ¼ teaspoon salt
- ¾ cup granulated sugar
- ½ cup (1 stick) butter or margarine
- 2 tablespoons water
- 1½ cups (9 ounces) NESTLÉ® TOLL HOUSE® Semi-Sweet Chocolate Morsels, *divided*
- ½ teaspoon peppermint extract
- ½ teaspoon vanilla extract
- 2 large eggs

Frosting
- 1 container (16 ounces) prepared vanilla frosting
- 1 tube (4½ ounces) chocolate decorating icing

For Brownies

PREHEAT oven to 350°F. Grease 9-inch square baking pan.

COMBINE flour, baking soda and salt in small bowl. Combine sugar, butter and water in medium saucepan. Bring *just to a boil* over medium heat, stirring constantly; remove from heat. (Or, combine sugar, butter and water in medium, microwave-safe bowl. Microwave on HIGH (100%) power for 3 minutes, stirring halfway through cooking time.) Stir until smooth.

ADD *1 cup* morsels, peppermint extract and vanilla extract; stir until smooth. Add eggs, one at a time, stirring well after each addition. Stir in flour mixture and *remaining* morsels. Spread into prepared baking pan.

BAKE for 20 to 30 minutes or until center is set. Cool completely (center will sink) in pan on wire rack.

For Frosting

SPREAD vanilla frosting over brownie. Squeeze chocolate icing in parallel lines over frosting. Drag wooden pick through chocolate icing to feather. Let stand until frosting is set. Cut into bars. *Makes about 16 brownies*

HERSHEY'S WHITE CHIP BROWNIES

4 eggs
1¼ cups sugar
½ cup (1 stick) butter or margarine, melted
2 teaspoons vanilla extract
1⅓ cups all-purpose flour
⅔ cup HERSHEY'S Cocoa
1 teaspoon baking powder
½ teaspoon salt
2 cups (12-ounce package) HERSHEY'S Premier White Chips

1. Heat oven to 350°F. Grease 13×9×2-inch baking pan.

2. Beat eggs in large bowl until foamy; gradually beat in sugar. Add butter and vanilla; beat until blended. Stir together flour, cocoa, baking powder and salt; add to egg mixture, beating until blended. Stir in white chips. Spread batter into prepared pan.

3. Bake 25 to 30 minutes or until brownies begin to pull away from sides of pan. Cool completely in pan on wire rack. Cut into squares.

Makes about 36 brownies

Tip: Brownies cut into different shapes can add interest to a plate of simple squares. Cut brownies into different size rectangles or make triangles by cutting them into 2- to 2½-inch squares; cut each square in half diagonally. To make diamond shapes, cut straight lines 1 or 1½ inches apart the length of the baking pan, then cut straight lines 1½ inches apart diagonally across the pan.

Prep Time: 15 minutes
Bake Time: 25 minutes
Cool Time: 2 hours

HERSHEY'S WHITE CHIP BROWNIES

FUDGY NUTTY COCONUT BARS

1 package (19 to 21 ounces) turtle brownie mix
½ cup vegetable oil
2 eggs
3 tablespoons water
1 cup peanut butter and milk chocolate chips*
1 cup semisweet chocolate chips
1⅓ cups flaked coconut
1 cup pecan pieces

*Butterscotch chips may be substituted for the peanut butter and milk chocolate chips.

1. Preheat oven to 350°F. Lightly grease 13×9-inch baking pan; set aside.

2. Combine brownie mix, oil, eggs and water in medium bowl; stir until well blended.

3. Spread batter evenly in prepared pan. Sprinkle with peanut butter and milk chocolate chips, semisweet chocolate chips, coconut and pecans; press firmly into batter.

4. Bake 24 to 27 minutes or until toothpick inserted 2 inches from side of pan comes out almost clean. Cool completely in pan on wire rack. Cut into bars.

Makes 2 dozen bars

Baking Tips

Always use the pan size called for in the recipe. Substituting a different pan will affect the brownies texture. A smaller pan will give the bars a more cakelike texture; a larger pan will produce a brownie with a drier texture.

FUDGY NUTTY COCONUT BARS

BROWNIE MINT SUNDAE SQUARES

1 (19.5- or 19.8-ounce family-size) package fudge brownie mix, plus ingredients to prepare mix

¾ cup coarsely chopped walnuts

1 (14-ounce) can EAGLE BRAND® Sweetened Condensed Milk (NOT evaporated milk)

2 teaspoons peppermint extract

4 to 6 drops green food coloring (optional)

2 cups (1 pint) whipping cream, whipped

½ cup miniature semisweet chocolate chips

    Hot fudge sauce or chocolate-flavored syrup (optional)

1. Line 13×9-inch baking pan with foil; grease. Prepare brownie mix as package directs; stir in walnuts. Spread in prepared pan. Bake as directed. Cool completely.

2. In large bowl, combine EAGLE BRAND®, peppermint extract and food coloring (optional). Fold in whipped cream and chocolate chips. Pour over brownie layer.

3. Cover; freeze 6 hours or until firm. To serve, lift brownies from pan with foil; cut into squares. Serve with hot fudge sauce (optional). Freeze leftovers.

Makes 10 to 12 servings

Baking Tips

Warm walnuts are easier to chop than cold or room temperature nuts. Place 1 cup of shelled nuts in a microwavable dish and heat on HIGH about 30 seconds or just until warm; chop as desired.

BROWNIE MINT SUNDAE SQUARES

BITTERSWEET PECAN BROWNIES WITH CARAMEL SAUCE

BROWNIES
- ¾ cup all-purpose flour
- ¼ teaspoon baking soda
- 4 squares (1 ounce each) bittersweet or unsweetened chocolate, coarsely chopped
- ½ cup (1 stick) plus 2 tablespoons I CAN'T BELIEVE IT'S NOT BUTTER!® Spread
- ¾ cup granulated sugar
- 2 eggs
- ½ cup chopped pecans

CARAMEL SAUCE
- ¾ cup firmly packed light brown sugar
- 6 tablespoons I CAN'T BELIEVE IT'S NOT BUTTER!® Spread
- ⅓ cup whipping or heavy cream
- ½ teaspoon apple cider vinegar or fresh lemon juice

For brownies, preheat oven to 325°F. Line 8-inch square baking pan with aluminum foil, then grease and flour foil; set aside.

In small bowl, combine flour and baking soda; set aside.

In medium microwave-safe bowl, microwave chocolate and I Can't Believe It's Not Butter!® Spread at HIGH (Full Power) 1 minute or until chocolate is melted; stir until smooth. With wooden spoon, beat in granulated sugar, then eggs. Beat in flour mixture. Evenly spread into prepared pan; sprinkle with pecans.

Bake 31 minutes or until toothpick inserted in center comes out clean. On wire rack, cool completely. To remove brownies, lift edges of foil. Cut brownies into 4 squares, then cut each square into 2 triangles.

For caramel sauce, in medium saucepan, bring brown sugar, I Can't Believe It's Not Butter! Spread and cream just to a boil over high heat, stirring frequently. Cook 3 minutes. Stir in vinegar. To serve, pour caramel sauce around brownie and top, if desired, with vanilla or caramel ice cream.

Makes 8 brownies

COCONUT CREAM CHEESE BROWNIES

- **1 cup (2 sticks) butter, melted**
- **4 eggs, divided**
- **1½ teaspoon WATKINS® Vanilla**
- **2¼ cups sugar, divided**
- **1¼ cups all-purpose flour**
- **½ cup WATKINS® Pure Cocoa**
- **½ teaspoon WATKINS® Baking Powder**
- **¼ teaspoon salt**
- **1 cup semisweet chocolate chips**
- **2 packages (8 ounces each) cream cheese**
- **2 teaspoons WATKINS® Coconut Extract**
- **¾ cup WATKINS® Coconut Dessert Mix**
- **2 tablespoons milk**

Preheat oven to 350°F. Grease 13×9-inch baking pan with WATKINS® Cooking Spray. Blend butter, 3 eggs and vanilla in large bowl. Combine 2 cups sugar, flour, cocoa, baking powder and salt in medium bowl; stir into egg mixture until well blended. Stir in chocolate chips. Set aside half of batter for topping. Spread remaining batter into prepared pan.

Beat cream cheese, remaining ¼ cup sugar and coconut extract in small bowl until smooth. Add dessert mix, remaining egg and milk; beat just until combined. Carefully spread filling over batter. Drop reserved batter by tablespoonfuls over filling. Cut through batter with knife to swirl, if desired. Bake for 35 to 40 minutes or until toothpick inserted into center comes out clean. Cool in pan on wire rack. Refrigerate until ready to serve.

Makes 3 dozen brownies

CHOCOLATEY ROCKY ROAD BROWNIES

Brownies

- 1 cup (2 sticks) butter
- 4 squares (1 ounce each) unsweetened chocolate
- 1½ cups granulated sugar
- 1 cup all-purpose flour
- 3 eggs
- 1½ teaspoons vanilla
- ½ cup chopped salted peanuts

Frosting

- ¼ cup (½ stick) butter
- 1 package (3 ounces) cream cheese
- 1 square (1 ounce) unsweetened chocolate
- ¼ cup milk
- 2¾ cups powdered sugar
- 1 teaspoon vanilla
- 2 cups miniature marshmallows
- 1 cup salted peanuts

Brownies

1. Preheat oven to 350°F. Grease 13×9-inch baking pan. Set aside.

2. Combine butter and chocolate in 3-quart saucepan. Cook over medium heat, stirring constantly, until melted, 5 to 7 minutes. Add granulated sugar, flour, eggs and vanilla; mix well. Stir in peanuts. Spread in prepared pan. Bake 20 to 25 minutes or until brownie starts to pull away from sides of pan. Cool completely in pan on wire rack.

Frosting

Combine butter, cream cheese, chocolate and milk in 2-quart saucepan. Cook over medium heat, stirring occasionally, until smooth, 6 to 8 minutes. Remove from heat; add powdered sugar and vanilla; beat until smooth. Stir in marshmallows and peanuts. Immediately spread over cooled brownies. Cool completely; cut into bars. Store leftovers covered in refrigerator.

Makes about 4 dozen brownies

CHOCOLATEY ROCKY ROAD BROWNIES·

Double-Decker Confetti Brownies

- ¾ cup (1½ sticks) butter or margarine, softened
- 1 cup granulated sugar
- 1 cup firmly packed light brown sugar
- 3 large eggs
- 1 teaspoon vanilla extract
- 2½ cups all-purpose flour, divided
- 2½ teaspoons baking powder
- ½ teaspoon salt
- ⅓ cup unsweetened cocoa powder
- 1 tablespoon butter or margarine, melted
- 1 cup "M&M's"® Semi-Sweet Chocolate Mini Baking Bits, divided

Preheat oven to 350°F. Lightly grease 13×9×2-inch baking pan; set aside. In large bowl cream ¾ cup butter and sugars until light and fluffy; beat in eggs and vanilla. In medium bowl combine 2¼ cups flour, baking powder and salt; blend into creamed mixture. Divide batter in half. Blend together cocoa powder and melted butter; stir into one half of the dough. Spread cocoa dough evenly into prepared baking pan. Stir remaining ¼ cup flour and ½ cup "M&M's"® Semi-Sweet Chocolate Mini Baking Bits into remaining dough; spread evenly over cocoa dough in pan. Sprinkle with remaining ½ cup "M&M's"® Semi-Sweet Chocolate Mini Baking Bits. Bake 25 to 30 minutes or until edges start to pull away from sides of pan. Cool completely. Cut into bars. Store in tightly covered container.

Makes 24 brownies

DOUBLE-DECKER CONFETTI BROWNIES

FUDGE TOPPED BROWNIES

2 cups sugar
1 cup (2 sticks) butter or margarine, melted
1 cup all-purpose flour
⅔ cup unsweetened cocoa
½ teaspoon baking powder
2 eggs
½ cup milk
3 teaspoons vanilla extract, divided
1 cup chopped nuts (optional)
2 cups (12 ounces) semisweet chocolate chips
1 (14-ounce) can EAGLE BRAND® Sweetened Condensed Milk
    (NOT evaporated milk)
Dash salt

1. Preheat oven to 350°F. In large bowl, combine sugar, butter, flour, cocoa, baking powder, eggs, milk and 1½ teaspoons vanilla; mix well. Stir in nuts (optional). Spread in greased 13×9-inch baking pan. Bake 40 minutes or until brownies begin to pull away from sides of pan.

2. In heavy saucepan, over low heat, melt chocolate chips with EAGLE BRAND®, remaining 1½ teaspoons vanilla and salt. Remove from heat. Immediately spread over hot brownies. Cool. Chill. Cut into bars. Store covered at room temperature.   *Makes 3 to 3½ dozen brownies*

FUDGE TOPPED BROWNIES

Easy Bar Cookies

CHEESECAKE COOKIE BARS

2 packages (18 ounces each) refrigerated chocolate chip cookie dough
2 packages (8 ounces each) cream cheese
½ cup sugar
2 eggs

1. Preheat oven to 350°F. Lightly grease 13×9-inch baking pan. Let both doughs stand at room temperature about 15 minutes.

2. Reserve three-fourths of one package of dough. Press remaining packages dough evenly onto bottom of prepared pan.

3. Combine cream cheese, sugar and eggs in large bowl. Beat with electric mixer at medium speed until well blended and smooth. Spread cream cheese mixture over dough in pan. Break reserved three-fourths package of dough into small pieces; sprinkle over cream cheese mixture.

4. Bake 35 minutes or until center is almost set. Cool completely in pan on wire rack. Store leftovers covered in refrigerator.

Makes about 2 dozen bars

CHEESECAKE COOKIE BARS

Jammy Wedges

　　1 package (18 ounces) refrigerated sugar cookie dough
　¼ cup granulated sugar
　　1 egg
　　3 tablespoons blackberry jam
　　　Powdered sugar
　　　Additional blackberry jam (optional)

1. Preheat oven to 350°F. Lightly grease 9-inch glass pie plate; line bottom of plate with waxed paper. Let dough stand at room temperature about 15 minutes.

2. Combine dough, granulated sugar and egg in large bowl. Beat with electric mixer at medium speed until well blended. (Dough will be sticky.) Spread dough in prepared pie plate; smooth top. Stir jam in small bowl until smooth. Dot top of dough with jam. Swirl jam into dough using tip of knife.

3. Bake 30 to 35 minutes or until edges are light brown and center is set. Cool at least 5 minutes in pie plate on wire rack.

4. Sprinkle with powdered sugar and cut into wedges just before serving. Serve with additional jam, if desired.　　　　*Makes 8 to 10 wedges*

Baking Tips

These super fast wedges make a great afternoon snack or even a sweet treat for breakfast.

JAMMY WEDGES

Shortbread Turtle Cookie Bars

1¼ cups (2½ sticks) butter, softened, divided
1 cup all-purpose flour
1 cup uncooked old-fashioned oats
1¼ cups packed brown sugar, divided
1 teaspoon ground cinnamon
¼ teaspoon salt
1½ cups chopped pecans
4 squares (1 ounce each) white chocolate, finely chopped
6 squares (1 ounce each) bittersweet or semisweet chocolate, finely chopped

1. Preheat oven to 350°F.

2. Beat ½ cup butter in large bowl with electric mixer at medium speed 2 minutes or until light and fluffy. Add flour, oats, ¾ cup brown sugar, cinnamon and salt; beat at low speed until coarse crumbs form. Pat firmly onto bottom of ungreased 13×9-inch baking pan. Set aside.

3. Heat remaining ¾ cup butter and ¾ cup brown sugar in heavy medium saucepan over medium-high heat, stirring constantly until butter melts. Bring mixture to a boil; cook 1 minute without stirring. Remove from heat; stir in pecans. Pour over crust.

4. Bake 18 to 22 minutes on center rack of oven or until caramel begins to bubble. Immediately sprinkle with white and bittersweet chocolates; swirl (do not spread) with knife after 45 seconds to 1 minute or when slightly softened. Cool completely in pan on wire rack; cut into 2×1-inch bars.

Makes about 4½ dozen bars

SHORTBREAD TURTLE COOKIE BARS

OATMEAL DATE BARS

2 packages (18 ounces each) refrigerated oatmeal raisin cookie dough
2½ cups uncooked old-fashioned oats, divided
2 packages (8 ounces each) chopped dates
1 cup water
½ cup sugar
1 teaspoon vanilla

1. Preheat oven to 350°F. Lightly grease 13×9-inch baking pan. Let both doughs stand at room temperature about 15 minutes.

2. Combine three-fourths of one package of dough and 1 cup oats in medium bowl; beat until well blended. Set aside.

3. Combine remaining packages dough and remaining 1½ cups oats in large bowl. Beat with electric mixer at medium speed until well blended. Press dough evenly onto bottom of prepared pan. Bake 10 minutes.

4. Meanwhile, combine dates, water and sugar in medium saucepan; bring to a boil over high heat. Boil 3 minutes; remove from heat and stir in vanilla. Spread date mixture evenly over partially baked crust; sprinkle evenly with reserved oats mixture.

5. Bake 25 to 28 minutes or until bubbly. Cool completely in pan on wire rack.

Makes about 2 dozen bars

OATMEAL DATE BARS

Champion Cherry Bars

    1 cup (2 sticks) margarine, softened
    ¾ cup granulated sugar
    ¾ cup firmly packed brown sugar
    2 eggs
    1 teaspoon vanilla extract
 2¼ cups all-purpose flour
    1 teaspoon baking powder
    1 (12-ounce) package vanilla milk chips
    2 cups dried tart cherries
    1 cup coarsely chopped pecans

Combine margarine, granulated sugar and brown sugar in a large mixing bowl. Beat with an electric mixer on medium speed 3 to 4 minutes, or until well blended. Add eggs and vanilla.

Combine flour and baking powder; gradually add to margarine mixture. Stir in vanilla milk chips, dried cherries and pecans. Spread dough evenly in greased 15×10×1-inch baking pan.

Bake in a preheated 350°F oven 20 minutes, or until light golden brown. Do not overbake. Let cool in pan, then cut into bars. Store in an airtight container. These bars freeze well.   *Makes 4 dozen bars*

Favorite recipe from **Cherry Marketing Institute**

Rich Chocolate Chip Toffee Bars

2⅓ cups all-purpose flour
⅔ cup packed light brown sugar
¾ cup (1½ sticks) butter or margarine
1 egg, lightly beaten
2 cups (12-ounce package) HERSHEY'S Semi-Sweet Chocolate Chips, divided
1 cup coarsely chopped nuts
1 can (14 ounces) sweetened condensed milk (not evaporated milk)
1⅓ cups (8-ounce package) HEATH® BITS 'O BRICKLE® Almond Toffee Bits, divided

1. Heat oven to 350°F. Grease 13×9×2-inch baking pan.

2. Combine flour and brown sugar in large bowl. Cut butter into flour mixture with pastry blender or two knives until mixture resembles coarse crumbs. Add egg; mix well. Stir in 1½ cups chocolate chips and nuts; set aside 1½ cups mixture.

3. Press remaining crumb mixture onto bottom of prepared pan. Bake 10 minutes. Pour sweetened condensed milk evenly over hot crust. Set aside ¼ cup toffee bits. Sprinkle remaining toffee bits over sweetened condensed milk. Sprinkle reserved crumb mixture and remaining ½ cup chocolate chips over top.

4. Bake 25 to 30 minutes or until golden brown. Top with reserved ¼ cup toffee bits. Cool completely in pan on wire rack. Cut into bars.

Makes 48 bars

Peanut Butter Cheesecake Bars

1 package (18¼ ounces) yellow cake mix with pudding in the mix
½ cup (1 stick) butter, softened, cut into small pieces
2 packages (8 ounces each) cream cheese, softened
1 cup chunky peanut butter
3 eggs
1¼ cups sugar
1 cup salted roasted peanuts
Melted chocolate (optional)

1. Preheat oven to 325°F. Combine cake mix and butter in large bowl. Beat with electric mixer at medium speed just until crumbly. Remove 1 cup mixture. Press remaining mixture evenly into ungreased 13×9-inch baking pan to form crust. Bake 10 minutes; cool on wire rack.

2. Combine cream cheese and peanut butter in large bowl. Beat with electric mixer at medium speed until fluffy. Beat in eggs, one at a time, scraping down side of bowl occasionally. Gradually beat in sugar until light. Spoon filling over cooled crust.

3. Combine reserved cake mix mixture and peanuts; spread evenly over filling.

4. Bake 45 minutes or until cake is just set and toothpick inserted into center comes out clean. Remove from oven; cool at room temperature 30 minutes. Chill at least 2 hours before serving. Drizzle with melted chocolate, if desired.   *Makes 24 bars*

Peanut Butter Cheesecake Bars

Raspberry Bars

1¼ cups all-purpose flour
¾ cup sugar, divided
½ cup (1 stick) butter or margarine, cut into ½-inch pieces
1 egg, beaten
2 egg whites
¾ cup chopped pecans
¾ cup raspberry jelly or jam

1. Preheat oven to 350°F. Grease 9-inch square baking pan; set aside.

2. Combine flour and ¼ cup sugar in medium bowl. Cut in butter with pastry blender or two knives until fine crumbs form. Add egg; mix with fork until dough holds together. Pat into smooth ball. Firmly press dough evenly into bottom of prepared pan. Bake 20 to 25 minutes or until crust is pale golden in color.

3. Meanwhile, beat egg whites in medium bowl with electric mixer at high speed until soft peaks form. Fold in remaining ½ cup sugar and pecans.

4. Spread jelly evenly over warm crust. Spread egg white mixture over jelly.

5. Bake 25 minutes more or until top is lightly browned. Cool in pan about 1 hour. Cut into bars.   *Makes about 16 bars*

RASPBERRY BARS

PM Snack Bars

3 tablespoons creamy peanut butter
2 tablespoons molasses
2 egg whites
2 tablespoons ground flaxseed
4 cups crisp rice cereal
½ cup sliced almonds
1 ounce bittersweet chocolate, melted and cooled

1. Preheat over to 350°F. Spray 9×9-inch baking pan with nonstick cooking spray. Place peanut butter in small microwavable bowl; microwave 30 seconds at LOW (30% power) or until peanut butter is melted. Stir in molasses; cool.

2. Place egg whites in blender with flaxseed. Process until foamy. Pour into large bowl. Add peanut butter mixture; stir until smooth. Stir in cereal and almonds; stir until cereal is evenly coated.

3. Press cereal mixture into prepared pan. Bake 20 to 25 minutes or until browned on top. Cool completely in pan on wire rack. Cut into 16 bars. Drizzle melted chocolate over bars.   *Makes 16 bars*

Baking Tips

Flaxseed can be found in health-food stores and some supermarkets. Due to its high fat content it should be stored in the refrigerator or freezer for up to 6 months.

PM Snack Bars

Peanut Butter Cookie Bars

1 package (18 ounces) refrigerated peanut butter cookie dough
1 can (14 ounces) sweetened condensed milk
¼ cup all-purpose flour
¼ cup peanut butter
1 cup peanut butter chips
1 cup chopped peanuts

1. Preheat oven to 350°F. Lightly grease 13×9-inch baking pan. Let dough stand at room temperature about 15 minutes.

2. Press dough evenly onto bottom of prepared pan. Bake 10 minutes.

3. Meanwhile, combine sweetened condensed milk, flour and peanut butter in medium bowl. Beat with electric mixer at medium speed until well blended. Spoon over partially baked crust. Sprinkle evenly with peanut butter chips and peanuts; press down lightly.

4. Bake 15 to 18 minutes or until center is set. Cool completely in pan on wire rack.
Makes about 2 dozen bars

PEANUT BUTTER COOKIE BARS

Chocolate Dream Bars

2¼ cups all-purpose flour, divided
1 cup (2 sticks) butter, softened
¾ cup powdered sugar
⅓ cups unsweetened cocoa powder
2 cups granulated sugar
4 eggs, beaten
4 squares (1 ounce each) unsweetened baking chocolate, melted
Additional powdered sugar for garnish (optional)

1. Preheat oven to 350°F.

2. Combine 2 cups flour, butter, powdered sugar and cocoa in large bowl. Beat with electric mixer at medium speed until well blended and stiff dough forms. Press firmly into ungreased 13×9-inch baking dish. Bake 15 to 20 minutes or just until set. Do not overbake.

3. Meanwhile, combine remaining ¼ cup flour and granulated sugar in medium bowl. Stir in eggs and melted chocolate; beat until blended. Pour over crust.

4. Bake 25 minutes or until toothpick inserted into center comes out clean. Cool completely in pan on wire rack. Sprinkle with powdered sugar, if desired. Cut into bars.   *Makes 3 dozen bars*

Tip: To make a powdered sugar design on these bars, place a stencil, doily or strips of paper over the tops of the bars before dusting them with powdered sugar. Carefully lift off the stencil, doily or paper strips, holding firmly by the edges and pulling straight up.

WHITE CHIP LEMON STREUSEL BARS

1 can (14 ounces) sweetened condensed milk (not evaporated milk)
½ cup lemon juice
1 teaspoon freshly grated lemon peel
2 cups (12-ounce package) HERSHEY₅S Premier White Chips, divided
1 cup packed light brown sugar
⅔ cup butter or margarine, softened
1½ cups all-purpose flour
1½ cups regular rolled or quick-cooking oats
¾ cup toasted pecan pieces*
1 teaspoon baking powder
½ teaspoon salt
1 egg
½ teaspoon shortening

To toast pecans: Heat oven to 350°F. Spread pecans in thin layer in shallow baking pan. Bake, stirring occasionally, 7 to 8 minutes or until golden brown; cool.

1. Heat oven to 350°F. Lightly grease 13×9×2-inch baking pan. Combine sweetened condensed milk, lemon juice and lemon peel in medium bowl; set aside. Measure out ¼ cup and ⅓ cup white chips; set aside. Add remaining white chips to lemon mixture.

2. Beat brown sugar and butter with electric mixer on medium speed in large bowl until well blended. Stir together flour, oats, pecans, baking powder and salt; add to butter mixture, blending well. Set aside 1⅔ cups oats mixture. Add egg to remaining oats mixture, blending until crumbly; press onto bottom of prepared pan. Gently spoon lemon mixture on top, spreading evenly. Add reserved ⅓ cup white chips to reserved oats mixture. Sprinkle over lemon layer, pressing down lightly.

3. Bake 20 to 25 minutes or until lightly browned. Cool in pan on wire rack. Place remaining ¼ cup white chips and shortening in small microwave-safe bowl. Microwave at HIGH (100%) 30 seconds or until chips are melted and mixture is smooth when stirred. Drizzle over baked bars. Allow drizzle to set; cut into bars.   *Makes 36 bars*

LAYERED COOKIE BARS

¾ cup (1½ sticks) butter or margarine
1¾ cups vanilla wafer crumbs
6 tablespoons HERSHEY'S Cocoa
¼ cup sugar
1 can (14 ounces) sweetened condensed milk
1 cup HERSHEY'S Semi-Sweet Chocolate Chips
¾ cup HEATH® BITS 'O BRICKLE® Toffee Bits
1 cup chopped walnuts

1. Heat oven to 350°F. Melt butter in 13×9×2-inch baking pan in oven. Combine crumbs, cocoa and sugar; sprinkle over butter.

2. Pour sweetened condensed milk evenly on top of crumbs. Top with chocolate chips and toffee bits, then nuts; press down firmly.

3. Bake 25 to 30 minutes or until lightly browned. Cool completely in pan on wire rack. Chill, if desired. Cut into bars. Store covered at room temperature. *Makes about 36 bars*

LAYERED COOKIE BARS

Cocoa Bottom Banana Pecan Bars

    1 cup sugar
    ½ cup (1 stick) butter, softened
    5 ripe bananas, mashed
    1 egg
    1 teaspoon vanilla
 1½ cups all-purpose flour
    1 teaspoon baking powder
    1 teaspoon baking soda
    ½ teaspoon salt
    ½ cup chopped pecans
    ¼ cup unsweetened cocoa powder

1. Preheat oven to 350°F. Grease 13×9-inch baking pan; set aside.

2. Combine sugar and butter in large bowl. Beat with electric mixer at medium speed until creamy. Add bananas, egg and vanilla; beat until well blended. Combine flour, baking powder, baking soda and salt in medium bowl. Add to banana mixture; beat until well blended. Stir in pecans.

3. Divide batter in half. Stir cocoa into one half. Spread cocoa batter in prepared pan. Spread plain batter over cocoa batter; swirl with knife.

4. Bake 30 to 35 minutes or until edges are lightly browned and toothpick inserted into center comes out clean. Cool completely in pan on wire rack. Cut into squares.
Makes 15 to 18 bars

Cocoa Bottom Banana Pecan Bars

CHERRY CHEESECAKE SWIRL BARS

Crust
- 1⅔ cups crushed graham crackers (about 25 2½-inch square graham crackers)
- 6 tablespoons (¾ stick) unsalted butter, melted
- 3 tablespoons sugar

Cheesecake
- 2 packages (8 ounces each) cream cheese, softened
- ½ cup sugar
- 2 eggs
- 1 egg yolk
- ⅓ cup sour cream
- 1 tablespoon all-purpose flour
- ½ teaspoon almond extract
- 3 tablespoons strained cherry preserves, melted

1. Preheat oven to 325°F. For crust, combine graham crumbs, butter and sugar in 9-inch square baking pan until well combined. Press onto pan bottom. Bake 8 minutes or until set but not brown. Remove from oven; cool.

2. For cheesecake, beat cream cheese in medium bowl with electric mixer at medium speed, scraping down side of bowl as needed. Add sugar, beating until smooth, scraping down side of bowl as needed. Add eggs, yolk, sour cream, flour and almond extract, beating until well blended and scraping down side of bowl as needed. Pour over crust in pan.

3. Drizzle melted preserves in zigzag pattern over batter. Drag knife tip through batter and jam to make swirled pattern.

4. Place pan in larger pan filled with 2 inches of water. Bake 45 minutes or until knife inserted 1 inch from edge comes out clean. Cut into squares.

Makes 16 bars

Variation: For flavor variety, substitute any seedless jam for the cherry preserves. Use vanilla extract instead of almond extract.

CHOCOLATE PEANUTTY CRUMBLE BARS

- ½ **cup (1 stick) butter or margarine**
- 1 **cup all-purpose flour**
- ¾ **cup instant oats, uncooked**
- ⅓ **cup firmly packed brown sugar**
- ½ **teaspoon baking soda**
- ½ **teaspoon vanilla extract**
- 4 **SNICKERS® Bars (2.07 ounces each), cut into 8 slices each**

Preheat oven to 350°F. Grease bottom of 8-inch square baking pan. Melt butter in large saucepan. Remove from heat and stir in flour, oats, brown sugar, baking soda and vanilla. Blend until crumbly. Press ⅔ of mixture into prepared pan. Arrange SNICKERS® Bar slices in pan about ½ inch from edge of pan. Finely crumble remaining mixture over sliced SNICKERS® Bars. Bake for 25 minutes or until edges are golden brown. Cool in pan on wire rack. Cut into bars or squares to serve. *Makes 24 bars*

Baking Tips

Cookies, brownies and bars make great gifts. Place them in a paper-lined tin or on a decorative plate; cover with plastic wrap and tie with a colorful ribbon. For a special touch, include the recipe.

CHOCOLATE WALNUT BARS

1½ cups all-purpose flour
¾ cup sugar
¾ cup (1½ sticks) cold butter, cut into pieces
1 can (14 ounces) sweetened condensed milk (not evaporated milk)
1 cup semisweet chocolate chips
1 egg
½ teaspoon vanilla
2 cups walnuts, toasted, chopped

1. Preheat oven to 350°F. Combine flour and sugar in large bowl; cut in butter using pastry blender or two knives until crumbly. Press firmly on bottom of ungreased 13×9-inch baking pan. Bake 20 minutes or until lightly browned.

2. Meanwhile, combine sweetened condensed milk and chocolate chips in medium saucepan over low heat. Cook and stir until chocolate is melted and mixture is smooth. Remove from heat; let cool slightly.

3. Add egg and vanilla to chocolate mixture; stir until well blended. Stir in walnuts. Spread chocolate mixture over partially baked crust. Bake 25 minutes or until center is set. Cool completely in pan on wire rack.

Makes 2 dozen bars

Chocolate Walnut Bars

S'MORE BARS

1 package (18 ounces) refrigerated chocolate chip cookie dough
¼ cup graham cracker crumbs
3 cups mini marshmallows
½ cup semisweet or milk chocolate chips
2 teaspoons shortening

1. Preheat oven to 350°F. Grease 13×9-inch baking pan. Press dough into prepared pan. Sprinkle evenly with graham cracker crumbs.

2. Bake 10 to 12 minutes or until edges are golden brown. Sprinkle with marshmallows. Bake 2 to 3 minutes or until marshmallows are puffed. Cool completely in pan on wire rack.

3. Combine chocolate chips and shortening in small resealable food storage bag; seal. Microwave on HIGH 1 minute; knead bag lightly. Microwave on HIGH for additional 30-second intervals until chips and shortening are completely melted and smooth, kneading bag after each 30-second interval. Cut off small corner of bag. Drizzle over bars. Refrigerate 5 to 10 minutes or until chocolate is set. Cut into bars.   *Makes 3 dozen bars*

S'MORE BARS

JAM JAM BARS

1 package (18¼ ounces) yellow or white cake mix with pudding in the mix
½ cup (1 stick) butter, melted
1 cup apricot preserves or raspberry jam
1 package (11 ounces) peanut butter and milk chocolate chips

1. Preheat oven to 350°F. Lightly spray 13×9-inch baking pan with nonstick cooking spray.

2. Pour cake mix into large bowl; stir in melted butter until well blended. (Dough will be lumpy.) Remove ½ cup dough and set aside. Press remaining dough evenly into prepared pan. Spread preserves in thin layer over dough in pan.

3. Place chips in medium bowl. Stir in reserved dough until well mixed. (Dough will remain in small lumps evenly distributed throughout chips.) Sprinkle mixture evenly over preserves.

4. Bake 20 minutes or until lightly browned and bubbling at edges. Cool completely in pan on wire rack.   *Makes 24 bars*

JAM JAM BARS

Cheery Cherry Brownies

¾ cup all-purpose flour
½ cup sugar substitute
½ cup unsweetened cocoa powder
¼ teaspoon baking soda
½ cup evaporated skimmed milk
⅓ cup butter, melted
¼ cup cholesterol-free egg substitute
¼ cup honey
1 teaspoon vanilla
½ (15½-ounce) can pitted tart red cherries, drained and halved

1. Preheat oven to 350°F. Grease 11×7-inch baking pan; set aside.

2. Stir together flour, sugar substitute, cocoa and baking soda in large mixing bowl. Add milk, butter, egg substitute, honey and vanilla. Stir just until blended.

3. Pour into prepared pan. Sprinkle cherries over top of chocolate mixture. Bake 13 to 15 minutes or until toothpick inserted into center comes out clean. Cool completely in pan on wire rack. Cut into 12 equal-size brownies. *Makes 12 brownies*

CHEERY CHERRY BROWNIE

COOKIE PIZZA

1 (18-ounce) package refrigerated sugar cookie dough
2 cups (12 ounces) semisweet chocolate chips
1 (14-ounce) can **EAGLE BRAND®** Sweetened Condensed Milk
  (NOT evaporated milk)
2 cups candy-coated milk chocolate pieces
2 cups miniature marshmallows
½ cup peanuts

1. Preheat oven to 375°F. Divide cookie dough in half; press each half onto ungreased 12-inch pizza pans. Bake 10 minutes or until golden. Remove from oven.

2. In medium saucepan, melt chocolate chips with EAGLE BRAND®. Spread over crusts. Sprinkle with chocolate pieces, marshmallows and peanuts.

3. Bake 4 minutes or until marshmallows are lightly toasted. Cool. Cut into wedges.   *Makes 2 pizzas (24 servings)*

Prep Time: 15 minutes
Bake Time: 14 minutes

COOKIE PIZZA

Ooey-Gooey Caramel Peanut Butter Bars

1 package (18¼ ounces) yellow cake mix *without* pudding in the mix
1 cup uncooked quick-cooking oats
⅔ cup creamy peanut butter
1 egg, slightly beaten
2 tablespoons milk
1 package (8 ounces) cream cheese, softened
1 jar (12¼ ounces) caramel ice cream topping
1 cup semisweet chocolate chips

1. Preheat oven to 350°F. Lightly grease 13×9-inch baking pan.

2. Combine cake mix and oats in large bowl. Cut in peanut butter with pastry blender or two knives until mixture is crumbly.

3. Blend egg and milk in small bowl. Add to peanut butter mixture; stir just until combined. Reserve 1½ cups mixture. Press remaining peanut butter mixture into prepared pan.

4. Beat cream cheese in small bowl with electric mixer at medium speed until fluffy. Add caramel topping; beat just until combined. Carefully spread over peanut butter layer in pan. Break up reserved peanut butter mixture into small pieces; sprinkle over cream cheese layer. Sprinkle with chocolate chips.

5. Bake about 30 minutes or until nearly set in center. Cool completely on wire rack.   *Makes 24 bars*

OOEY-GOOEY CARAMEL PEANUT BUTTER BARS

CONVERSATION HEART CEREAL TREATS

20 large marshmallows
2 tablespoons margarine or butter
3 cups frosted oat cereal with marshmallow bits
12 large conversation hearts

1. Line 8- or 9-inch square pan with aluminum foil, leaving 2-inch overhangs on 2 sides. Generously grease or spray with nonstick cooking spray.

2. Melt marshmallows and margarine in medium saucepan over medium heat 3 minutes or until melted and smooth, stirring constantly. Remove from heat.

3. Add cereal; stir until completely coated. Spread in prepared pan; press evenly onto bottom using greased rubber spatula. Press heart candies into top of treats while still warm, evenly spacing to allow 1 heart per bar. Let cool 10 minutes. Using foil overhangs as handles, remove treats from pan. Cut into 12 bars.

Makes 12 bars

Prep Time: 10 minutes
Cook Time: 10 minutes
Cool Time: 10 minutes

Baking Tips

Be creative when making these gooey cereal treats. Substitute candy-coated chocolate pieces, red cinnamon candies or multi-colored chewy fruit pieces for conversation hearts. Add candies to marshmallow mixture with cereal.

CONVERSATION HEART CEREAL TREATS

GRANOLA RAISIN BARS

1 package (18¼ ounces) yellow cake mix with pudding in the mix, divided
½ cup (1 stick) butter, melted, divided
1 egg
4 cups granola cereal with raisins

1. Preheat oven to 350°F. Lightly spray 13×9-inch baking pan with nonstick cooking spray. Reserve ½ cup cake mix; set aside.

2. Combine remaining cake mix, 4 tablespoons melted butter and egg in large bowl; stir until well blended. (Dough will be thick and sticky.) Spoon dough into prepared pan. Cover with plastic wrap and press dough evenly into pan, using plastic wrap to keep hands from sticking to dough.

3. Bake 8 minutes. Meanwhile, combine reserved cake mix, granola cereal and remaining 4 tablespoons melted butter in medium bowl; stir until well blended. Spread mixture evenly over partially baked bars.

4. Return pan to oven; bake 15 to 20 minutes or until edges are lightly browned. Cool completely on wire rack. *Makes 15 bars*

WINTER WONDERLAND SNOWMEN BROWNIES

¾ cup HERSHEY'S Cocoa or HERSHEY'S SPECIAL DARK® Cocoa
½ teaspoon baking soda
⅔ cup butter or margarine, melted and divided
½ cup boiling water
2 cups sugar
2 eggs
1 teaspoon vanilla extract
1½ cups all-purpose flour
1⅔ cups (10-ounce package) REESE'S® Peanut Butter Chips
    Powdered sugar (optional)

1. Heat oven to 350°F. Line 13×9×2-inch baking pan with foil; grease foil.

2. Stir together cocoa and baking soda in large bowl; stir in ⅓ cup melted butter. Add boiling water; stir until mixture thickens. Stir in sugar, eggs, vanilla and remaining ⅓ cup butter; stir until smooth. Add flour; stir until blended. Stir in peanut butter chips. Pour into prepared pan.

3. Bake 35 to 40 minutes or until brownies begin to pull away from sides of foil. Cool completely in pan. Cover; refrigerate until firm. Remove from pan; remove foil. Cut into snowmen shapes with cookie cutters or cut into squares. Just before serving, sprinkle with powdered sugar, if desired.

Makes about 12 large brownies or 36 squares

Two-Tone Cheesecake Bars

> **2 cups finely crushed chocolate creme-filled sandwich cookies (about 24 cookies)**
> **3 tablespoons butter or margarine, melted**
> **3 (8-ounce) packages cream cheese, softened**
> **1 (14-ounce) can EAGLE BRAND® Sweetened Condensed Milk (NOT evaporated milk)**
> **3 eggs**
> **2 teaspoons vanilla extract**
> **2 (1-ounce) squares unsweetened chocolate, melted**
> **Chocolate Glaze (recipe follows)**

1. Preheat oven to 300°F. In medium bowl, combine cookie crumbs and butter; press firmly on bottom of ungreased 13×9-inch baking pan.

2. In large bowl, beat cream cheese until fluffy. Gradually beat in EAGLE BRAND® until smooth. Add eggs and vanilla; mix well. Pour half the batter evenly over prepared crust. Stir melted chocolate into remaining batter; pour evenly over plain batter.

3. Bake 55 to 60 minutes or until set. Cool. Top with Chocolate Glaze. Chill. Cut into bars. Store leftovers covered in refrigerator.

Makes 2 to 3 dozen bars

Prep Time: 15 minutes

Chocolate Glaze

> **2 (1-ounce) squares unsweetened chocolate**
> **2 tablespoons butter or margarine**
> **Pinch salt**
> **1¾ cups confectioners' sugar**
> **3 tablespoons hot water or cream**

In heavy saucepan over low heat, melt chocolate and butter with salt. Remove from heat. Add confectioners' sugar and hot water or cream; mix well. Immediately spread over cheesecake.

Makes about 1 cup

TWO-TONE CHEESECAKE BARS

CRISPY COOKIE TREATS

1 package (18 ounces) refrigerated bite size miniature chocolate chip cookie dough (40 count)
½ cup (1 stick) butter
½ teaspoon ground cinnamon
1 package (16 ounces) miniature marshmallows
4 cups crisp rice cereal
2 cups unsweetened granola

1. Bake cookies according to package directions. Reserve 24 cooled cookies. Coarsely chop remaining 16 cookies. Place chopped cookies in resealable food storage bag; seal bag. Freeze at least 1 hour.

2. Melt butter in large saucepan over medium heat; stir in cinnamon. Add marshmallows; cook and stir until melted and smooth. Remove from heat; let stand 10 minutes, stirring every few minutes.

3. Meanwhile, lightly grease 13×9-inch baking pan and rubber spatula. Combine cereal, granola and frozen chopped cookies in large bowl. Pour marshmallow mixture over cereal mixture; stir with spatula until well blended.

4. Press mixture into prepared pan; flatten into bars with lightly greased waxed paper or hands. Press reserved 24 cookies on top of bars, spacing evenly. Let stand at room temperature about 2 hours or until set. Cut into 2×2¼-inch bars.

Makes 2 dozen bars

CRISPY COOKIE TREATS

Brownie Gems

1 package DUNCAN HINES® Chocolate Lover's® Double Fudge Brownie Mix
2 eggs
2 tablespoons water
⅓ cup vegetable oil
28 miniature peanut butter cup or chocolate kiss candies
1 container of your favorite DUNCAN HINES® frosting

1. Preheat oven to 350°F. Spray (1¾-inch) mini-muffin pans with vegetable cooking spray or line with foil baking cups.

2. Combine brownie mix, fudge packet from mix, eggs, water and oil in large bowl. Stir with spoon until well blended, about 50 strokes. Drop 1 heaping teaspoonful of batter into each muffin cup; top with candy. Cover candy with more batter. Bake at 350°F for 15 to 17 minutes.

3. Cool 5 minutes. Carefully loosen brownies from pan. Remove to wire racks to cool completely. Frost and decorate as desired.

Makes 28 brownie gems

Baking Tips

Make these adorable brownies in advance. They can be frozen in an airtight container for up to 3 months. Just add them to packed lunches for a super treat!

BROWNIE GEMS

PEANUT BUTTER CUP BARS

1½ cups all-purpose flour
1 teaspoon baking powder
1 teaspoon salt
⅔ cup IMPERIAL® Spread, softened
2 cups sugar
4 eggs
1 cup semi-sweet chocolate chips, melted
½ cup SKIPPY® Creamy Peanut Butter

Preheat oven to 350°F. Grease 13×9-inch baking pan; set aside.

In medium bowl, combine flour, baking powder and salt; set aside.

In large bowl with electric mixer, beat Imperial Spread and sugar on medium-high speed until light and fluffy, about 5 minutes. Beat in eggs, scraping side occasionally. Gradually beat in flour mixture until blended. Remove 2 cups batter to medium bowl and stir in melted chocolate. Evenly spread batter into prepared pan. Add peanut butter to remaining batter in large bowl; beat until blended. Spoon over chocolate batter and spread into even layer.

Bake uncovered 35 minutes or until center is set. On wire rack, cool completely. To serve, cut into bars. *Makes 2 dozen bars*

Prep Time: 15 minutes
Bake Time: 35 minutes

RAISIN OATMEAL PIZZA COOKIE

¾ **cup butter or margarine, softened**
1 **cup packed brown sugar**
½ **cup granulated sugar**
¼ **cup milk**
1 **large egg**
1 **teaspoon vanilla**
1 **cup all-purpose flour**
1 **teaspoon cinnamon**
½ **teaspoon baking soda**
¼ **teaspoon salt**
3 **cups old-fashioned oats**
1 **cup SUN-MAID® Raisins**
1½ **cups white chocolate baking chips**
1 **package SUN-MAID® California or Mediterranean Apricots for "Pepperoni"**
1 **package SUN-MAID® Fruit Bits or Tropical Medley for pizza "topping"**

1. **HEAT** oven to 325°F. Grease two cookie sheets or pizza pans.

2. **BEAT** butter, brown sugar, granulated sugar, milk, egg and vanilla in a large bowl until well blended. Beat in flour, cinnamon, baking soda and salt.

3. **STIR** in oats and raisins.

4. **DIVIDE** dough in half and place on prepared pans. With floured hands, pat dough into 9-inch circles. Bake* 18 to 20 minutes until cookies are firm to the touch and golden brown. Let cool.

5. **PLACE** white baking chips in a microwave-safe bowl. Microwave* on MEDIUM power (50%) for about 2 minutes. Stir until chips are melted.

6. **SPREAD** chocolate on cookies. Immediately top with apricots and choice of dried fruit "toppings", pressing lightly into chocolate to hold in place. Cut into wedges. *Makes 2 large cookies*

Adult supervision suggested.

CRAZY CREATURE BROWNIES

1¼ cups granulated sugar
¾ cup (1½ sticks) butter or margarine
½ cup unsweetened cocoa powder
½ cup cholesterol-free egg substitute
1 teaspoon vanilla
½ teaspoon baking soda
½ teaspoon baking powder
1½ cups all-purpose flour
1 cup low-fat buttermilk
3 cups powdered sugar, sifted
⅓ cup orange juice, apple juice or fat-free milk
Food coloring (optional)

1. Preheat oven to 350°F. Line 15×10×1-inch jelly-roll pan with heavy-duty foil, extending foil over edges. Spray foil with nonstick cooking spray. Combine granulated sugar, butter and cocoa powder in large saucepan. Cook over low heat, stirring frequently, until butter is melted. Remove from heat.

2. Cool sugar mixture 5 minutes. Stir in egg substitute. Add vanilla, baking soda and baking powder; mix well. Alternately add flour and buttermilk, stirring until well blended after each addition. Spread into prepared pan. Bake 20 to 22 minutes or until toothpick inserted into center comes out clean. Cool completely.

3. Use foil to lift brownie out of pan. Remove foil; place brownie on cutting board. Cut in shapes with 2- to 3-inch animal shaped cookie cutters. Place on wire rack over wax paper.

4. Combine powdered sugar and orange juice in small bowl. Tint with food coloring, if desired. Spread over brownies. Decorate as desired. Let stand about 20 minutes or until dry.   *Makes 20 brownies*

Prep Time: 10 minutes
Bake Time: 20 minutes
Cool Time: 1 hour

CRAZY CREATURE BROWNIES

BURIED CHERRY BARS

 1 jar (10 ounces) maraschino cherries
 1 package (18¼ ounces) devil's food cake mix *without* pudding in the mix
 1 cup (2 sticks) butter, melted
 1 egg
 ½ teaspoon almond extract
 1½ cups semisweet chocolate chips
 ¾ cup sweetened condensed milk
 ½ cup chopped pecans

1. Preheat oven to 350°F. Lightly grease 13×9-inch baking pan. Drain maraschino cherries, reserving 2 tablespoons juice. Cut cherries into quarters.

2. Combine cake mix, butter, egg and almond extract in large bowl; mix well. (Batter will be very thick.) Spread batter in prepared pan. Lightly press cherries into batter.

3. Combine chocolate chips and sweetened condensed milk in small saucepan. Cook over low heat, stirring constantly, until chocolate melts. Stir in reserved cherry juice. Spread chocolate mixture over cherries in pan; sprinkle with pecans.

4. Bake 35 minutes or until almost set in center. Cool completely in pan on wire rack. Cut into bars.   *Makes 24 bars*

Baking Tips

For a fun and different shape, cut brownies into triangles. First cut brownies into bars as directed in step 4, then cut diagonally across each brownies to create triangles.

BURIED CHERRY BARS

"Everything but the Kitchen Sink" Bar Cookies

1 package (18 ounces) refrigerated chocolate chip cookie dough
1 jar (7 ounces) marshmallow creme
½ cup creamy peanut butter
1½ cups toasted corn cereal
½ cup miniature candy-coated chocolate pieces

1. Preheat oven to 350°F. Grease 13×9-inch baking pan. Press dough into prepared pan. Bake 13 minutes.

2. Remove from oven. Drop teaspoonfuls of marshmallow creme and peanut butter over hot cookie base. Bake 1 minute.

3. Carefully spread marshmallow creme and peanut butter. Sprinkle with cereal and chocolate pieces. Bake 7 minutes.

4. Cool completely in pan on wire rack. Cut into 2-inch bars.

Makes 3 dozen bars

"EVERYTHING BUT THE KITCHEN SINK" BAR COOKIES

Space Dust Bars

- **1 package (12 ounces) white chocolate chips**
- **⅓ cup butter**
- **2 cups graham cracker crumbs**
- **1 cup chopped pecans**
- **2 cans (12 ounces each) apricot dessert and pastry filling**
- **1 cup sweetened flaked coconut**
  Additional sweetened flaked coconut or powdered sugar (optional)

1. Preheat oven to 350°F. Grease 13×9-inch baking pan. Combine white chocolate chips and butter in medium saucepan; cook and stir over low heat until melted and smooth. Remove from heat; stir in graham cracker crumbs and pecans. Let cool 5 minutes.

2. Press half of crumb mixture onto bottom of prepared pan. Bake 10 minutes or until light brown. Spread apricot filling evenly over hot crust. Combine coconut with remaining crumb mixture; sprinkle evenly over top of apricot filling.

3. Bake 20 to 25 minutes or until light golden brown. Cool completely in pan on wire rack. Sprinkle with additional coconut or powdered sugar, if desired. Cut into bars. *Makes 1½ dozen bars*

SPACE DUST BARS

BRRRROWNIE CATS

1 cup (2 sticks) unsalted butter
4 squares (1 ounce each) unsweetened chocolate
1½ cups sugar
3 eggs
1 cup all-purpose flour
¼ teaspoon salt
Black frosting, sprinkles and decors

1. Preheat oven to 350°F. Grease 13×9-inch baking pan. Melt butter and chocolate in top of double boiler*, stirring occasionally.

2. Transfer chocolate mixture to large bowl. Stir in sugar until well blended. Beat in eggs with electric mixer at medium speed, one at a time. Stir in flour and salt.

3. Spread batter into prepared pan. Bake 20 to 25 minutes or just until firm. Cool completely on wire rack.

4. Cut brownies into cat shapes using Halloween cookie cutters. Decorate as desired.   *Makes about 2 dozen brownies*

Or, place unwrapped chocolate squares in small microwavable bowl. Microwave at HIGH 1 to 1½ minutes, stirring after 1 minute.

CONTENTS

Sunrise Starters

PUMPKIN RAISIN MUFFINS

¾ cup canned pumpkin
6 tablespoons vegetable oil
1 egg
2 egg whites
1 tablespoon light molasses
1 teaspoon vanilla
1¼ cups all-purpose flour
1 cup EQUAL® SPOONFUL*
½ cup raisins
1 tablespoon baking powder
1 teaspoon ground cinnamon
½ teaspoon ground nutmeg
½ teaspoon ground ginger
¼ teaspoon salt

*May substitute 24 packets EQUAL® sweetener.

• Combine pumpkin, oil, egg and egg whites, molasses and vanilla. Stir in combined flour, Equal®, raisins, baking powder, cinnamon, nutmeg, ginger and salt just until all ingredients are moistened. Fill paper-lined 2½-inch muffin cups about ¾ full.

• Bake in preheated 375°F oven 18 to 20 minutes or until wooden pick inserted into centers comes out clean. Cool in pan on wire rack 2 to 3 minutes. Remove muffins from pan and cool completely on wire rack.

Makes 12 muffins

PUMPKIN RAISIN MUFFIN

COFFEE CUP MUFFINS

¾ cup less 2 tablespoons all-purpose flour
¼ cup plus 2 tablespoons sugar substitute*
½ teaspoon baking powder
½ teaspoon ground cinnamon
¼ teaspoon baking soda
½ cup egg substitute
2 tablespoons unsweetened applesauce
1 tablespoon canola oil
½ teaspoon vanilla
1 cup shredded carrots
2 tablespoons raisins

* This recipes was tested with sucralose-based sugar substitute.

1. Preheat oven to 400°F. Lightly spray 2 (8-ounce) ovenproof coffee cups with nonstick cooking spray; set aside.

2. Combine flour, sugar substitute, baking powder, cinnamon and baking soda in medium bowl.

3. Whisk together egg substitute, applesauce, oil and vanilla in another medium bowl about 1 minute or until smooth. Add carrots and raisins; stir until well blended. Add flour mixture to egg mixture; stir about 1 minute or until smooth.

4. Spoon batter into prepared coffee cups. Push shredded carrots into batter to smooth tops.

5. Place cups on baking sheet; bake on center oven rack 20 minutes or until toothpick inserted into centers comes out clean.

6. Cool 5 minutes. Serve in cup or run knife around edges to loosen and slide out onto serving plate. *Makes 2 muffins*

COFFEE CUP MUFFINS

HONEY MUFFINS

1 can (8 ounces) DOLE® Crushed Pineapple
1½ cups wheat bran cereal (not flakes)
⅔ cup buttermilk
1 egg, lightly beaten
⅓ cup chopped pecans or walnuts
3 tablespoons vegetable oil
½ cup honey, divided
⅔ cup whole wheat flour
½ teaspoon baking soda
⅛ teaspoon salt

Combine undrained crushed pineapple, cereal and buttermilk in large bowl. Let stand 10 minutes until cereal has absorbed liquid. Stir in egg, pecans, oil and ¼ cup honey. Combine flour, baking soda and salt in small bowl. Stir into bran mixture until just moistened. Spoon one-half batter into 6 prepared cups,* filling to the top.

Microwave at HIGH (100%) for 3½ to 4 minutes, rotating pan half turn after 1½ minutes. Muffins are done when they look dry and set on top. Remove from oven; immediately spoon 1 teaspoon of remaining honey over each muffin. Remove to cooling rack after honey has been absorbed. Repeat procedure with remaining batter and honey. Serve warm.

Makes 12 muffins

*Line six microwavable muffin cups or six 6-ounce microwavable custard cups with double thickness paper baking cups. (Outer cup will absorb moisture so inner cup sticks to cooked muffin.)

HONEY MUFFINS

CRANBERRY PECAN MUFFINS

1¾ cups all-purpose flour
½ cup packed light brown sugar
2½ teaspoons baking powder
½ teaspoon salt
¾ cup milk
¼ cup (½ stick) butter, melted
1 egg, beaten
1 cup chopped fresh cranberries
⅓ cup chopped pecans
1 teaspoon grated lemon peel

1. Preheat oven to 400°F. Grease or paper-line 36 mini (1¾-inch) muffin cups.

2. Combine flour, brown sugar, baking powder and salt in large bowl. Combine milk, butter and egg in small bowl until blended; stir into flour mixture just until moistened. Fold in cranberries, pecans and lemon peel. Spoon into prepared muffin cups, filling almost full.

3. Bake 15 to 17 minutes or until toothpick inserted into centers comes out clean. Remove from pans. Cool on wire racks.   *Makes 36 mini muffins*

Baking Tips

Remove muffins from their cups immediately after baking and cool them on a wire rack. They are best when served warm. Stored in an airtight plastic bag, muffins will stay fresh for several days.

CRANBERRY PECAN MUFFINS

Breakfast Muffins

¾ cup all-purpose flour
¾ cup whole wheat flour
½ cup quick or old-fashioned oats
½ cup firmly packed brown sugar
⅓ cup toasted wheat germ
2 tablespoons flax seeds, finely ground (optional)
1½ teaspoons baking powder
1 teaspoon ground cinnamon
½ teaspoon salt
¼ teaspoon ground nutmeg
1 cup fat-free (skim) milk
½ cup vegetable oil
1 egg, beaten
½ cup raisins
½ cup dark or semisweet chocolate chips *or* ⅓ cup cinnamon chips

1. Preheat oven to 350°F. Lightly grease 12 (2¾-inch) muffin cups.

2. Combine flours, oats, sugar, wheat germ, flax seed, if desired, baking powder, cinnamon, salt and nutmeg in medium bowl. Combine milk, oil and egg in small bowl until well blended; add milk mixture to flour mixture. Stir until almost blended; stir in raisins and chocolate chips.

3. Fill muffin cups three-fourths full with batter. Bake 20 to 22 minutes or until toothpick inserted into centers comes out clean. Cool in pan on wire rack 15 minutes. Remove muffins to wire rack. Serve warm or at room temperature. *Makes 12 muffins*

APPLE RAISIN WALNUT MUFFINS

2 cups all-purpose flour
¾ cup sugar
2 teaspoons baking powder
1 teaspoon ground cinnamon
½ teaspoon baking soda
½ teaspoon salt
¼ teaspoon ground nutmeg
¾ cup plus 2 tablespoons milk
⅓ cup butter, melted
2 eggs, beaten
1 cup chopped dried apples
½ cup golden raisins
½ cup chopped walnuts

1. Preheat oven to 350°F. Grease 6 jumbo (3½-inch) muffin cups. Combine flour, sugar, baking powder, cinnamon, baking soda, salt and nutmeg in large bowl.

2. Combine milk, butter and eggs in small bowl. Stir into flour mixture just until blended. Gently fold in apples, raisins and walnuts. Fill prepared muffin cups three-fourths full.

3. Bake 25 to 30 minutes or until toothpick inserted into centers comes out clean. Cool in pan 2 minutes; remove muffins to wire rack. Serve warm or at room temperature. *Makes 6 jumbo muffins*

MARMALADE MUFFINS

 2 cups all-purpose flour
 2 teaspoons baking powder
 ¾ teaspoon salt
 1 cup (2 sticks) unsalted butter, softened
 1½ cups sugar
 2 eggs
 1½ teaspoons vanilla
 1 cup orange marmalade, plus more for topping
 1 cup buttermilk

1. Preheat oven to 350°F. Line 18 (2½-inch) muffin cups with paper baking cups.

2. Sift flour, baking powder and salt in medium bowl; set aside.

3. Combine butter and sugar in large bowl. Beat with electric mixer at high speed until light and fluffy, about 5 minutes. Add eggs one at a time and beat until blended. Add vanilla and mix well. Fold in half dry mixture just until moistened. Mix in 1 cup marmalade and remaining dry mixture.

4. Stir in buttermilk; do not overmix. Fill baking cups three-fourths full. Bake 20 to 25 minutes or until edges are light brown and toothpick inserted into centers comes out clean. Top with additional marmalade.

Makes 18 muffins

Baking Tips

To easily fill muffin cups, place batter in a 4-cup glass measure. Fill each cup three-fourths full. Use plastic spatula to control the flow of the batter.

MARMALADE MUFFINS

Jelly Donut Muffins

1¼ **cups nonfat milk**
¼ **cup Dried Plum Purée (recipe follows) or prepared dried plum butter**
1 **egg**
2 **tablespoons vegetable oil**
1 **teaspoon vanilla**
2 **cups all-purpose flour**
⅓ **cup sugar**
1 **tablespoon baking powder**
1 **teaspoon ground cardamom or cinnamon**
½ **teaspoon salt**
¼ **cup strawberry jam**

Preheat oven to 425°F. Coat twelve 2¾-inch (⅓-cup capacity) muffin cups with vegetable cooking spray. In large bowl, beat first five ingredients until well blended. In medium bowl, combine flour, sugar, baking powder, cardamom and salt. Add to milk mixture; mix just until blended. Spoon about half of batter into prepared muffin cups. Top each with 1 teaspoon jam and remaining batter, covering jam completely. Bake 15 to 20 minutes or until springy to the touch. Cool in pans 10 minutes. Remove to wire rack to cool slightly. Serve warm.   *Makes 12 muffins*

Dried Plum Purée: Combine 1⅓ cups (8 ounces) pitted dried plums and 6 tablespoons hot water in container of food processor or blender. Pulse on and off until dried plums are finely chopped and smooth. Store leftovers in a covered container in the refrigerator for up to two months. Makes 1 cup.

Favorite recipe from **California Dried Plum Board**

JELLY DONUT MUFFINS

MOCHA-MACADAMIA NUT MUFFINS

1¼ cups all-purpose flour
⅔ cup granulated sugar
2½ tablespoons unsweetened cocoa powder
1 teaspoon baking soda
¼ teaspoon salt
⅔ cup buttermilk*
3 tablespoons butter, melted
1 egg, beaten
1 tablespoon instant coffee granules dissolved in 1 tablespoon hot water
¾ teaspoon vanilla
½ cup coarsely chopped macadamia nuts
   Powdered sugar (optional)

Soured fresh milk can be substituted for buttermilk. To sour milk, combine 2 teaspoons lemon juice plus enough milk to equal ⅔ cup. Stir; let stand 5 minutes before using.

1. Preheat oven to 400°F. Lightly grease 12 (2½-inch) muffin cups or line with paper baking cups.

2. Combine flour, sugar, cocoa, baking soda and salt in large bowl. Combine buttermilk, butter, egg, coffee mixture and vanilla in medium bowl; beat with electric mixer at medium speed until blended. Stir buttermilk mixture into flour mixture just until dry ingredients are moistened. Stir in macadamia nuts. Spoon batter evenly into prepared muffin cups.

3. Bake 13 to 17 minutes or until toothpick inserted into centers comes out clean. Cool in pan on wire rack 5 minutes. Remove from pan to wire rack; cool 10 minutes. Sprinkle with powdered sugar, if desired.

Makes 12 muffins

Gift Idea: Line a rustic basket with a colorful new placemat or dishtowel. Place the muffins in the basket and wrap the basket with cellophane. Secure the top with a multitude of ribbon and attach a gift tag.

Mocha-Macadamia Nut Muffins

Peanut Butter & Jam Muffins

2 cups all-purpose flour
2 teaspoons baking powder
1 teaspoon baking soda
2 eggs
½ cup no-sugar-added natural peanut butter
¾ cup thawed frozen unsweetened apple juice concentrate
¼ cup milk
¼ cup (½ stick) butter, melted
½ cup chopped salted peanuts
6 tablespoons strawberry jam

1. Preheat oven to 350°F. Grease 12 (2½-inch) muffin cups or line with paper baking cups; set aside.

2. Combine dry ingredients in medium bowl; set aside. Beat together eggs and peanut butter in separate medium bowl until smooth. Blend in apple juice concentrate, milk and butter. Add to dry ingredients; mix just until dry ingredients are moistened. Stir in peanuts. Spoon half of batter evenly into prepared muffin cups. Drop 1½ teaspoons strawberry fruit spread into center of each cup; cover with remaining batter.

3. Bake 18 minutes or until golden brown. Cool in pan on wire rack 5 minutes. Remove from pan; cool. Serve warm or at room temperature.

Makes 12 muffins

PEANUT BUTTER & JAM MUFFINS

CINNAMON SPICED MUFFINS

1½ cups all-purpose flour
¾ cup sugar, divided
2 teaspoons baking powder
½ teaspoon salt
½ teaspoon ground nutmeg
½ teaspoon ground coriander
½ teaspoon ground allspice
½ cup milk
⅓ cup plus ¼ cup butter, melted
1 egg
1 teaspoon ground cinnamon

1. Preheat oven to 400°F. Grease 36 (1¾-inch) mini-muffin cups.

2. Combine flour, ½ cup sugar, baking powder, salt, nutmeg, coriander and allspice in large bowl. Combine milk, ⅓ cup butter and egg in small bowl; stir into flour mixture just until moistened. Spoon evenly into prepared muffin cups.

3. Bake 10 to 13 minutes or until edges are lightly browned and toothpick inserted into centers comes out clean. Remove from pan.

4. Meanwhile, combine remaining ¼ cup sugar and cinnamon in shallow dish. Dip warm muffin tops in ¼ cup melted butter, then in cinnamon-sugar mixture. Serve warm.

Makes 36 mini muffins

CINNAMON SPICED MUFFINS

TROPICAL TREAT MUFFINS

2 cups all-purpose flour
⅓ cup plus 1 tablespoon sugar, divided
1 tablespoon baking powder
1 teaspoon grated lemon peel
½ teaspoon salt
¾ cup (4 ounces) dried papaya, finely diced
½ cup coarsely chopped banana chips
½ cup chopped macadamia nuts
¼ cup flaked coconut
½ cup milk
½ cup (1 stick) butter, melted
¼ cup sour cream
1 egg, beaten

1. Preheat oven to 400°F. Grease 12 (2½-inch) or 6 (4-inch) jumbo muffin cups or line with paper baking cups.

2. Combine flour, ⅓ cup sugar, baking powder, lemon peel and salt in large bowl. Combine papaya, banana chips, macadamia nuts and coconut in small bowl; stir in 1 tablespoon flour mixture until well coated. Combine milk, butter, sour cream and egg in another small bowl until blended; stir into flour mixture just until moistened. Fold in fruit mixture. Spoon evenly into prepared muffin cups. Sprinkle remaining 1 tablespoon sugar over tops of muffins.

3. Bake 15 to 20 minutes for standard muffins, 25 to 30 minutes for jumbo muffins, or until toothpick inserted into centers comes out clean. Remove from pan. Cool on wire rack. *Makes 12 regular-size or 6 jumbo muffins*

TROPICAL TREAT MUFFINS

SNACKING SURPRISE MUFFINS

Muffins
 1½ cups all-purpose flour
 ½ cup sugar
 1 cup fresh or frozen blueberries
 2½ teaspoons baking powder
 1 teaspoon ground cinnamon
 ¼ teaspoon salt
 1 egg, beaten
 ⅔ cup buttermilk
 ¼ cup butter, melted
 3 tablespoons peach preserves

Topping
 1 tablespoon sugar
 ¼ teaspoon ground cinnamon

1. Preheat oven to 400°F. Line 12 (2½-inch) muffin cups with paper baking cups; set aside.

2. For muffins, combine flour, ½ cup sugar, blueberries, baking powder, 1 teaspoon cinnamon and salt in medium bowl. Combine egg, buttermilk and butter in small bowl. Add to flour mixture; mix just until moistened.

3. Spoon about 1 tablespoon batter into each muffin cup. Drop scant teaspoonful of preserves into center of batter in each cup; top with remaining batter.

4. For topping, combine 1 tablespoon sugar and ¼ teaspoon cinnamon in small bowl; sprinkle evenly over tops of batter.

5. Bake 18 to 20 minutes or until lightly browned. Remove muffins to wire rack to cool completely.   *Makes 12 muffins*

SNACKING SURPRISE MUFFINS

Double Chocolate Zucchini Muffins

2⅓ cups all-purpose flour
1¼ cups sugar
⅓ cup unsweetened cocoa powder
2 teaspoons baking powder
1½ teaspoons ground cinnamon
1 teaspoon baking soda
½ teaspoon salt
1 cup sour cream
½ cup vegetable oil
2 eggs, beaten
¼ cup milk
1 cup milk chocolate chips
1 cup shredded zucchini

1. Preheat oven to 400°F. Grease 12 jumbo (3½-inch) muffin cups.

2. Combine flour, sugar, cocoa, baking powder, cinnamon, baking soda and salt in large bowl. Combine sour cream, oil, eggs and milk in small bowl until blended; stir into flour mixture just until moistened. Fold in chocolate chips and zucchini. Spoon into prepared muffin cups, filling half full.

3. Bake 25 to 30 minutes until toothpick inserted into centers comes out clean. Cool in pan on wire racks 5 minutes. Remove from pan. Cool completely on wire rack. Store tightly covered at room temperature.

Makes 12 jumbo muffins

DOUBLE CHOCOLATE ZUCCHINI MUFFINS

BLUEBERRY CHEESECAKE MUFFINS

1 package (8 ounces) cream cheese, softened
1 cup plus 1 tablespoon sugar substitute, divided
2 eggs, divided
1 teaspoon grated lemon peel
1 teaspoon vanilla
¾ cup bran flakes cereal
½ cup all-purpose flour
½ cup soy flour
2 teaspoons baking powder
¼ teaspoon salt
¾ cup milk
3 tablespoons melted butter
4 tablespoons no-sugar-added blueberry fruit spread
½ teaspoon ground cinnamon

1. Preheat oven to 350°F. Spray 12 (2½-inch) muffin cups with nonstick cooking spray.

2. Beat cream cheese in medium bowl with electric mixer at high speed until smooth. Beat in ¾ cup sugar substitute, 1 egg, lemon peel and vanilla.

3. Combine cereal, flours, ¼ cup sugar substitute, baking powder and salt in medium bowl. Whisk milk, butter and remaining egg in small bowl until blended; pour over cereal mixture. Gently mix just until blended.

4. Spoon about 2 tablespoons batter into each muffin cup. Spread 1 teaspoon fruit spread over batter. Spread cream cheese mixture over fruit spread. Combine remaining 1 tablespoon sugar substitute and cinnamon; sprinkle mixture evenly over cream cheese mixture.

5. Bake 30 to 35 minutes or until toothpicks inserted into centers come out clean. Cool muffins 10 minutes in pan on wire rack. Remove muffins from pan. Serve warm or at room temperature. Refrigerate leftover muffins.

Makes 12 muffins

BLUEBERRY CHEESECAKE MUFFINS

GINGERBREAD STREUSEL RAISIN MUFFINS

   1 cup raisins
  ½ cup boiling water
  ⅓ cup margarine or butter, softened
  ¾ cup GRANDMA'S® Molasses (Unsulphured)
   1 egg
   2 cups all-purpose flour
1½ teaspoons baking soda
   1 teaspoon ground cinnamon
   1 teaspoon ground ginger
  ½ teaspoon salt

Topping
  ⅓ cup all-purpose flour
  ¼ cup firmly packed brown sugar
  ¼ cup chopped nuts
   3 tablespoons margarine or butter
   1 teaspoon cinnamon

Preheat oven to 375°F. Grease bottoms only of 12 muffin cups or line with paper baking cups. In small bowl, cover raisins with boiling water; let stand 5 minutes. In large bowl, beat ⅓ cup margarine and molasses until fluffy. Add egg; beat well. Stir in 2 cups flour, baking soda, 1 teaspoon cinnamon, ginger and salt. Blend just until dry ingredients are moistened. Gently stir in raisins and water. Fill prepared muffin cups ¾ full. For topping, combine all ingredients in small bowl. Sprinkle over muffins.

Bake 20 to 25 minutes or until toothpick inserted in centers comes out clean. Cool 5 minutes; remove from pan. Serve warm.   *Makes 12 muffins*

GINGERBREAD STREUSEL RAISIN MUFFINS

Baby Bran Muffins with Citrus Spread

Bran Muffins
- 1 cup whole bran cereal
- 1 cup milk
- 1 egg, beaten
- 2 tablespoons butter, melted
- 1 cup all-purpose flour
- ¼ cup packed brown sugar
- 2½ teaspoons baking powder
- ½ teaspoon baking soda
- ¼ teaspoon salt
- ¼ teaspoon ground cinnamon
- ¼ cup currants

Citrus Spread
- 1 package (8 ounces) cream cheese, softened
- 3 tablespoons orange juice
- 1 teaspoon granulated sugar

1. Preheat oven to 375°F. Spray 24 miniature (1¾-inch) muffin pan cups with nonstick cooking spray. Set aside.

2. For muffins, combine cereal, milk, egg and butter in large bowl. Set aside 10 minutes. Combine flour, brown sugar, baking powder, baking soda, salt and cinnamon in large bowl. Add to bran mixture, stirring just until blended. Fold in currants.

3. Spoon batter into prepared muffin cups filling three-fourths full. Bake 15 minutes or until firm when lightly pressed. Let muffins stand 1 minute; remove to wire racks to cool.

4. To prepare Citrus Spread, combine cream cheese, orange juice and granulated sugar in large bowl. Beat with electric mixer at high speed 1 minute or until cream cheese is light and fluffy. Split open muffins and spread lightly with Citrus Spread. *Makes 24 muffins*

Tip: Leftover muffins can be frozen in resealable plastic food storage bag. Reheat in preheated 325°F oven for 5 minutes.

Baby Bran Muffins with Citrus Spread

APPLE BUTTER SPICE MUFFINS

½ **cup sugar**
1 **teaspoon ground cinnamon**
¼ **teaspoon ground nutmeg**
⅛ **teaspoon ground allspice**
½ **cup pecans or walnuts, chopped**
2 **cups all-purpose flour**
2 **teaspoons baking powder**
¼ **teaspoon salt**
1 **cup milk**
¼ **cup vegetable oil**
1 **egg**
¼ **cup apple butter**

1. Preheat oven to 400°F. Grease 12 (2½-inch) muffin cups or line with paper baking cups.

2. Combine sugar, cinnamon, nutmeg and allspice in large bowl. Toss 2 tablespoons sugar mixture with pecans in small bowl; set aside. Add flour, baking powder and salt to remaining sugar mixture.

3. Combine milk, oil and egg in medium bowl. Stir into flour mixture just until moistened.

4. Spoon 1 tablespoon batter into each prepared muffin cup. Spoon 1 teaspoon apple butter into each cup. Spoon remaining batter evenly over apple butter. Sprinkle reserved pecan mixture over each muffin. Bake 20 to 25 minutes or until light brown and toothpick inserted into centers comes out clean. Immediately remove from pan; cool on wire rack 10 minutes. Serve warm or cool completely. *Makes 12 muffins*

Apple Butter Spice Muffins

Orange Coconut Muffins

¾ cup all-purpose flour
¾ cup whole wheat flour
⅔ cup toasted wheat germ
½ cup sugar
½ cup flaked coconut
1½ teaspoons baking soda
½ teaspoon salt
1 cup sour cream
2 eggs
1 can (11 ounces) mandarin oranges, drained
½ cup chopped nuts

Preheat oven to 400°F. Butter 12 (2½-inch) muffin cups.

Combine flours, wheat germ, sugar, coconut, baking soda and salt in large bowl. Blend sour cream, eggs and oranges in small bowl; stir into flour mixture just until moistened. Fold in nuts. Spoon into prepared muffin cups, filling ¾ full.

Bake 18 to 20 minutes or until wooden pick inserted in center comes out clean. Remove from pan. Cool on wire rack.   *Makes 12 muffins*

Favorite recipe from **Wisconsin Milk Marketing Board**

Baking Tips

Don't stir muffin batter too much—overmixing will make the muffins tough. There should still be lumps in the batter; these will disappear during baking.

ORANGE COCONUT MUFFINS

CRANBERRY SUNSHINE MUFFINS

1½ cups all-purpose flour
½ cup **SPLENDA® No Calorie Sweetener, Granular**
2 teaspoons baking powder
1 teaspoon baking soda
½ teaspoon ground cinnamon
1 cup chopped fresh or frozen cranberries
¼ cup chopped walnuts
½ cup orange juice
¼ cup nonfat sour cream
1 egg or equivalent in egg substitute
1 tablespoon plus 1 teaspoon reduced-calorie margarine

1. Preheat oven to 375°F. Spray 8 muffin pan cups with butter-flavored cooking spray or line with paper liners.

2. In large bowl, combine flour, SPLENDA®, baking powder, baking soda and cinnamon. Stir in cranberries and walnuts.

3. In small bowl, combine orange juice, sour cream, egg and margarine. Add liquid mixture to dry mixture. Stir gently just to combine. Evenly spoon batter into prepared muffin cups.

4. Bake for 15 to 20 minutes or until toothpick inserted into centers comes out clean. Cool in pan on wire rack for 5 minutes. Remove muffins from pan and continue cooling on wire rack. *Makes 8 muffins*

Tip: Fill unused muffin cups with water. It protects the muffin pan and ensures even baking.

CRANBERRY SUNSHINE MUFFINS

Fruitful Treats

CHUNKY APPLE MOLASSES MUFFINS

 2 cups all-purpose flour
¼ cup sugar
 1 tablespoon baking powder
 1 teaspoon ground cinnamon
¼ teaspoon salt
 1 Fuji apple, peeled, cored and finely chopped
½ cup milk
¼ cup vegetable oil
¼ cup molasses
 1 large egg

1. Heat oven to 450°F. Lightly grease 8 (3-inch) muffin pan cups. In large bowl, combine flour, sugar, baking powder, cinnamon and salt. Add apple and stir to distribute evenly.

2. In small bowl, beat together milk, oil, molasses and egg. Stir into dry ingredients and mix just until blended. Fill muffin pan cups with batter. Bake 5 minutes. Reduce heat to 350°F; bake 12 to 15 minutes longer or until centers of muffins spring back when gently pressed. Cool in pan 5 minutes. Remove muffins from pan and cool slightly; serve warm.

Makes 8 (3-inch) muffins

Favorite recipe from **Washington Apple Commission**

CHUNKY APPLE MOLASSES MUFFINS

BERRY BRAN MUFFINS

2 cups dry bran cereal
1¼ cups fat-free (skim) milk
½ cup packed brown sugar
¼ cup vegetable oil
1 egg, lightly beaten
1 teaspoon vanilla
1¼ cups all-purpose flour
1 tablespoon baking powder
¼ teaspoon salt
1 cup fresh or frozen blueberries (partially thawed if frozen)

1. Preheat oven to 350°F. Line 12 (2½-inch) muffin cups with paper baking cups.

2. Mix cereal and milk in medium bowl. Let stand 5 minutes to soften. Add brown sugar, oil, egg and vanilla. Beat well. Combine flour, baking powder and salt in large bowl. Stir in cereal mixture just until dry ingredients are moistened. Gently fold in berries.

3. Fill prepared muffin cups almost to top. Bake 20 to 25 minutes (25 to 30 if using frozen berries) or until toothpick inserted into centers comes out clean. Serve warm.   *Makes 12 muffins*

Baking Tips

Try substituting fresh or frozen raspberries for the blueberries in this recipe. Or, even better, use ½ cup of each kind of berry for a berrylicious treat!

BERRY BRAN MUFFINS

CRANBERRY CHEESECAKE MUFFINS

1 package (3 ounces) cream cheese, softened
4 tablespoons sugar, divided
1 cup reduced-fat (2%) milk
⅓ cup vegetable oil
1 egg
1 package (about 15 ounces) cranberry quick bread mix

1. Preheat oven to 400°F. Grease 12 (2½-inch) muffin cups.

2. Beat cream cheese and 2 tablespoons sugar in small bowl until well blended; set aside.

3. Beat milk, oil and egg in large bowl until blended. Stir in quick bread mix just until dry ingredients are moistened.

4. Fill prepared muffin cups one-fourth full with batter. Drop 1 teaspoon cream cheese mixture into center of each cup. Spoon remaining batter over cream cheese mixture.

5. Sprinkle batter with remaining 2 tablespoons sugar. Bake 17 to 22 minutes or until light brown. Cool 5 minutes. Remove from muffin cups to wire rack to cool.

Makes 12 muffins

Prep Time: 15 minutes
Bake Time: 17 to 22 minutes

CRANBERRY CHEESECAKE MUFFINS

ORANGE MUFFINS

2 cups all-purpose flour
1 tablespoon grated orange peel
2 teaspoons baking powder
½ teaspoon baking soda
¼ teaspoon salt
¾ cup orange juice
¼ cup (½ stick) butter, melted
1 egg, beaten
2 tablespoons milk
1 teaspoon vanilla
  Whipped butter (optional)
  No-sugar-added orange marmalade fruit spread (optional)

1. Preheat oven to 400°F. Spray 12 (2½-inch) muffin cups with nonstick cooking spray or line with paper baking cups; set aside.

2. Combine flour, orange peel, baking powder, baking soda and salt in medium bowl. Combine orange juice, butter, egg, milk and vanilla in small bowl until blended; stir into flour mixture just until moistened.

3. Spoon batter into prepared muffin cups, filling each cup half full. Bake 18 to 20 minutes or until light brown. Let cool in pan on wire rack 5 minutes. Remove from pan; cool. Serve warm or at room temperature. Spread with whipped butter and marmalade, if desired.

Makes 12 muffins

PLUM OATMEAL MUFFINS

5 fresh California plums, halved and pitted, divided
2 cups all-purpose flour
1¾ cups rolled oats
¾ cup packed brown sugar
⅓ cup vegetable oil
1 egg
3 teaspoons baking powder
1 teaspoon salt
1 teaspoon vanilla
1 teaspoon grated orange peel

Spray nonstick cooking spray in muffin cups or use paper liners. Preheat oven to 350°F. Cut up 3 plums to measure 1 cup. Add to food processor or blender; process until smooth. Coarsely chop remaining 2 plums; set aside. Combine puréed plums, flour, oats, brown sugar, oil, egg, baking powder, salt, vanilla and orange peel. Stir until just blended. Stir in chopped plums. Fill prepared muffin cups ⅔ full. Bake 30 to 35 minutes or until wooden toothpick inserted in center comes out clean. *Makes 18 muffins*

Favorite recipe from **California Tree Fruit Agreement**

Baking Tips

For longer storage of these delicious muffins, wrap and freeze. To reheat, wrap frozen muffins in foil and heat in a 350°F oven for 15 to 20 minutes. For best flavor, use frozen muffins within one month.

APPLE STREUSEL MINI MUFFINS

¼ **cup chopped pecans**
2 **tablespoons brown sugar**
1 **tablespoon all-purpose flour**
2 **teaspoons butter, melted**
1 **package (7 ounces) apple-cinnamon muffin mix, plus ingredients to prepare mix**
½ **cup shredded peeled apple**

1. Preheat oven to 425°F. Spray 18 mini (1¾-inch) muffin cups with nonstick cooking spray.

2. Combine pecans, brown sugar, flour and butter in small bowl.

3. Prepare muffin mix according to package directions. Stir in apple. Fill each muffin cup two-thirds full. Sprinkle approximately 1 teaspoon pecan mixture on top of each muffin. Bake 12 to 15 minutes or until light brown. Cool slightly. Serve warm. *Makes 18 mini muffins*

Variation: For regular-size muffins, grease 6 (2½-inch) muffin cups. Prepare topping and batter as directed. Fill muffin cups two-thirds full. Sprinkle approximately 1 tablespoon pecan mixture on each muffin. Bake 18 to 20 minutes or until light brown. Makes 6 regular muffins.

Prep Time: 10 minutes
Bake Time: 12 to 15 minutes

APPLE STREUSEL MUFFINS

GINGERBREAD PEAR MUFFINS

1¾ cups all-purpose flour
⅓ cup sugar
2 teaspoons baking powder
¾ teaspoon ground ginger
¼ teaspoon baking soda
¼ teaspoon salt
¼ teaspoon ground cinnamon
⅓ cup milk
¼ cup vegetable oil
¼ cup light molasses
1 egg
1 medium pear, peeled, cored and finely chopped

1. Preheat oven to 375°F. Grease 12 (2½-inch) muffin cups or line with paper baking cups.

2. Sift flour, sugar, baking powder, ginger, baking soda, salt and cinnamon into large bowl.

3. Combine milk, oil, molasses and egg in medium bowl. Stir in pear. Stir milk mixture into flour mixture just until moistened.

4. Spoon evenly into prepared muffin cups, filling two-thirds full.

5. Bake 20 minutes or until toothpick inserted into centers comes out clean. Immediately remove from pan; cool on wire rack 10 minutes. Serve warm or at room temperature. *Makes 12 muffins*

GINGERBREAD PEAR MUFFINS

CHERRIES AND CREAM MUFFINS

2½ cups frozen unsweetened tart cherries, divided
1 cup granulated sugar
½ cup butter or margarine
2 eggs
1 teaspoon almond extract
½ teaspoon vanilla extract
2 cups all-purpose flour
2 teaspoons baking powder
½ teaspoon salt
½ cup light cream, half-and-half or milk

Cut cherries into halves while frozen. Set aside to thaw and drain. In large bowl, beat sugar and butter until light and fluffy. Add eggs, almond extract and vanilla, beating well. Crush ½ cup cherries with fork; stir into batter.

Combine flour, baking powder and salt. Fold half the flour mixture into batter with spatula, then half the cream. Fold in remaining flour and cream. Fold in remaining cherry halves. Portion batter evenly into 12 paper-lined or lightly greased muffin cups (2¾ inches in diameter). Sprinkle with additional sugar.

Bake in preheated 375°F oven 20 to 30 minutes or until golden brown.

Makes 12 muffins

Favorite recipe from **Cherry Marketing Institute**

BANANA CHOCOLATE CHIP MUFFINS

2 ripe, medium DOLE® Bananas
1 cup packed brown sugar
2 eggs
½ cup (1 stick) margarine, melted
1 teaspoon vanilla extract
2¼ cups all-purpose flour
2 teaspoons baking powder
½ teaspoon ground cinnamon
½ teaspoon salt
1 cup chocolate chips
½ cup chopped walnuts

• Purée bananas in blender; measure 1 cup for recipe. Beat bananas, sugar, eggs, margarine and vanilla in medium bowl until well blended.

• Combine flour, baking powder, cinnamon and salt in large bowl. Stir in chocolate chips and nuts. Make well in center of dry ingredients. Add banana mixture. Stir just until blended. Spoon into well greased 2½-inch muffin pan cups.

• Bake at 350°F 25 to 30 minutes or until toothpick inserted in centers comes out clean. Cool slightly; remove from pan and place on wire rack.

Makes 12 muffins

Prep Time: 20 minutes
Bake Time: 30 minutes

APRICOT-PEANUT BUTTER MUFFINS

1¾ cups **PILLSBURY BEST® All-Purpose or Unbleached Flour**
2½ tablespoons sugar
2½ teaspoons baking powder
 ¾ teaspoon salt
 ¼ cup **CRISCO® Shortening plus additional for greasing**
 ¼ cup **JIF® Creamy Peanut Butter**
 ¾ cup milk
 2 eggs
 2 tablespoons **SMUCKER'S® Apricot Preserves**

1. Preheat oven to 400°F. Grease 10 large muffin pan cups.

2. Combine flour, sugar, baking powder and salt in large bowl; cut in ¼ cup CRISCO Shortening and peanut butter with pastry blender or 2 knives.

3. Combine milk and eggs in small bowl; add all at once to dry ingredients. Stir just until dry ingredients are moistened.

4. Fill muffin cups ⅔ full. Spoon about ½ teaspoon preserves into center of each muffin.

5. Bake at 400°F for 25 minutes or until toothpick inserted near centers comes out clean.   *Makes 10 muffins*

Variation: Substitute your favorite SMUCKER'S® flavor in place of the apricot preserves in the above recipe. Experiment with strawberry or blackberry preserves or even apple butter.

APRICOT-PEANUT BUTTER MUFFINS

STRAWBERRY OAT MINI MUFFINS

    1 cup all-purpose flour
    ¾ cup uncooked oat bran cereal
    2½ teaspoons baking powder
    ½ teaspoon baking soda
    ⅛ teaspoon salt
    ¾ cup buttermilk
    ⅓ cup frozen apple juice concentrate, thawed
    ⅓ cup unsweetened applesauce
    ½ teaspoon vanilla
    ¾ cup diced strawberries
    ¼ cup chopped pecans

1. Preheat oven to 400°F. Spray 24 mini (1¾-inch) muffin cups with nonstick cooking spray.

2. Combine flour, cereal, baking powder, baking soda and salt in medium bowl. Whisk together buttermilk, apple juice concentrate, applesauce and vanilla in small bowl.

3. Stir buttermilk mixture into flour mixture just until dry ingredients are almost moistened. Fold strawberries and pecans into batter. *Do not overmix.*

4. Spoon batter into prepared muffin cups. Bake 17 to 18 minutes or until lightly browned and toothpick inserted into centers comes out clean. Cool in pan on wire rack 5 minutes. Remove muffins to racks. Serve warm or cool completely.   *Makes 24 mini muffins*

STRAWBERRY OAT MINI MUFFINS

PINEAPPLE-RAISIN MUFFINS

¼ cup finely chopped pecans
¼ cup packed light brown sugar
2 cups all-purpose flour
¼ cup granulated sugar
2½ teaspoons baking powder
¾ teaspoon salt
½ teaspoon ground cinnamon
6 tablespoons (¾ stick) cold butter, cut into pieces
½ cup raisins
1 can (8 ounces) crushed pineapple in juice, undrained
⅓ cup unsweetened pineapple juice
1 egg

1. Preheat oven to 400°F. Lightly grease 12 (2½-inch) muffin cups or line with paper baking cups.

2. Combine pecans and brown sugar in small bowl; set aside. Combine flour, granulated sugar, baking powder, salt and cinnamon in large bowl. Cut in butter with pastry blender or 2 knives until mixture resembles fine crumbs. Stir in raisins.

3. Combine crushed pineapple with juice, pineapple juice and egg in small bowl; stir until blended. Add to flour mixture; stir just until moistened. Spoon batter evenly into prepared muffin cups, filling two-thirds full. Sprinkle with pecan mixture.

4. Bake 20 to 25 minutes or until light brown and toothpicks inserted into centers come out clean. Immediately remove from pan; cool on wire rack 10 minutes. Serve warm or at room temperature.   *Makes 12 muffins*

PINEAPPLE-RAISIN MUFFINS

BLUEBERRY WHITE CHIP MUFFINS

2 cups all-purpose flour
½ cup granulated sugar
¼ cup packed brown sugar
2½ teaspoons baking powder
½ teaspoon salt
¾ cup milk
1 large egg, lightly beaten
¼ cup butter or margarine, melted
½ teaspoon grated lemon peel
2 cups (12-ounce package) NESTLÉ® TOLL HOUSE® Premier White Morsels,
    divided
1½ cups fresh or frozen blueberries
    Streusel Topping (recipe follows)

PREHEAT oven to 375°F. Paper-line 18 muffin cups.

COMBINE flour, granulated sugar, brown sugar, baking powder and salt in large bowl. Stir in milk, egg, butter and lemon peel. Stir in *1½ cups* morsels and blueberries. Spoon into prepared muffin cups, filling almost full. Sprinkle with Streusel Topping.

BAKE for 22 to 25 minutes or until wooden pick inserted in center comes out clean. Cool in pans for 5 minutes; remove to wire racks to cool slightly.

PLACE *remaining* morsels in small, *heavy-duty* resealable plastic food storage bag. Microwave on MEDIUM-HIGH (70%) power for 30 seconds; knead. Microwave at additional 10- to 15-second intervals, kneading until smooth. Cut tiny corner from bag; squeeze to drizzle over muffins. Serve warm.   *Makes 18 muffins*

Streusel Topping: **COMBINE** ⅓ cup granulated sugar, ¼ cup all-purpose flour and ¼ teaspoon ground cinnamon in small bowl. Cut in 3 tablespoons butter or margarine with pastry blender or two knives until mixture resembles coarse crumbs.

BLUEBERRY WHITE CHIP MUFFINS

Savory Goodies

CHEDDAR PEPPER MUFFINS

  2 cups all-purpose flour
  1 tablespoon baking powder
  1 tablespoon sugar
  1 teaspoon black pepper
  ½ teaspoon salt
1¼ cups milk
  ¼ cup vegetable oil
  1 egg
  1 cup (4 ounces) shredded sharp Cheddar cheese, divided

1. Preheat oven to 400°F. Grease 12 (2½-inch) muffin cups or line with paper baking cups.

2. Combine flour, baking powder, sugar, pepper and salt in large bowl. Combine milk, oil and egg in small bowl until blended. Stir into flour mixture just until dry ingredients are moistened. Fold in ¾ cup cheese. Spoon into prepared muffin cups. Sprinkle muffins with remaining ¼ cup cheese.

3. Bake 15 to 20 minutes or until light brown. Cool in pan on wire rack 5 minutes. Remove from pan; serve warm.   *Makes 12 muffins*

CHEDDAR PEPPER MUFFINS

GRANDMA'S® BRAN MUFFINS

2½ cups bran flakes, divided
1 cup raisins
1 cup boiling water
2 cups buttermilk
1 cup GRANDMA'S® Molasses
½ cup canola oil
2 eggs, beaten
2¾ cups all-purpose flour
2½ teaspoons baking soda
½ teaspoon salt

Heat oven to 400°F. In medium bowl, mix 1 cup bran flakes, raisins and water. Set aside. In large bowl, combine remaining ingredients. Stir in bran-raisin mixture. Pour into greased muffin pan cups. Fill ⅔ full and bake for 20 minutes. Remove muffins and place on rack to cool.   *Makes 48 muffins*

Baking Tips

A standard muffin cup measures
2½ inches in diameter and is
1½ inches deep. Also available are
jumbo muffin pans with cups
measuring 3¼ inches in diameter and
2 inches deep; and miniature pans
with cups measuring 1½ to 2 inches
in diameter and ¾ of an inch deep.

GRANDMA'S® BRAN MUFFINS

PESTO SURPRISE MUFFINS

2 cups all-purpose flour
3 tablespoons grated Parmesan cheese, divided
1 tablespoon baking powder
½ teaspoon salt
1 cup milk
¼ cup vegetable oil
1 egg
¼ cup prepared pesto sauce

1. Preheat oven to 400°F. Grease 12 (2½-inch) muffin cups or line with paper baking cups.

2. Combine flour, 2 tablespoons cheese, baking powder and salt in large bowl. Combine milk, oil and egg in small bowl; stir until blended. Stir into flour mixture just until moistened. *Do not overmix.* Spoon into prepared muffin cups, filling one-third full. Stir pesto sauce; spoon 1 teaspoon sauce into each muffin cup. Spoon remaining batter evenly over pesto sauce. Sprinkle remaining 1 tablespoon cheese evenly over batter.

3. Bake 25 to 30 minutes or until toothpicks inserted into centers come out clean. Cool in muffin pan on wire rack 5 minutes. Remove from pan and cool on wire rack 10 minutes.   *Makes 12 muffins*

PESTO SURPRISE MUFFINS

RASPBERRY-SESAME MUFFINS

1 cup nonfat milk
¼ cup Dried Plum Purée (recipe follows)
1 egg
2 cups all-purpose flour
⅓ cup sugar
3 tablespoons toasted sesame seeds, divided
1 tablespoon baking powder
½ teaspoon salt
2 tablespoons butter or margarine, melted
1 cup fresh or frozen raspberries

Preheat oven to 400°F. Coat twelve 2¾-inch (⅓-cup capacity) muffin cups with vegetable cooking spray. In large bowl, beat milk, dried plum purée and egg until well blended. In medium bowl, combine flour, sugar, 2 tablespoons sesame seeds, baking powder and salt. Add flour mixture to milk mixture; mix just until blended. Mix in butter; stir in raspberries. Spoon batter into prepared muffin cups, dividing equally. Sprinkle with remaining 1 tablespoon sesame seeds. Bake in center of oven 15 to 20 minutes or until lightly browned and springy to the touch. Remove muffins to wire rack to cool slightly. Serve warm.   *Makes 12 muffins*

Dried Plum Purée: Combine 1⅓ cups (8 ounces) pitted dried plums and 6 tablespoons hot water in container of food processor or blender. Pulse on and off until dried plums are finely chopped and smooth. Store leftovers in a covered container in the refrigerator for up to two months.

Favorite recipe from **California Dried Plum Board**

RASPBERRY-SESAME MUFFINS

SPICY CORN MUFFINS

1 cup low-fat buttermilk
1 tablespoon vegetable oil
1 egg white
1 serrano pepper,* minced
1 cup yellow cornmeal
⅓ cup all-purpose flour
1 tablespoon finely chopped fresh cilantro or parsley
1 teaspoon baking powder
½ teaspoon baking soda
¼ teaspoon salt
¼ teaspoon ground cumin
¼ teaspoon ground paprika

* Serrano peppers can sting and irritate the skin, so wear rubber gloves when handling peppers and do not touch your eyes.

1. Preheat oven to 400°F. Spray 6 jumbo (3½-inch) muffin cups with nonstick cooking spray; set aside.

2. Combine buttermilk, oil, egg white and serrano pepper in small bowl until smooth.

3. Combine cornmeal, flour, cilantro, baking powder, baking soda, salt, cumin and paprika in medium bowl; mix well. Make well in dry ingredients; pour in buttermilk mixture. Stir with fork just until dry ingredients are moistened.

4. Spoon batter evenly into prepared muffin cups. Bake 15 to 20 minutes or until toothpick inserted into centers comes out clean.　　*Makes 6 muffins*

SPICY CORN MUFFINS

GARDEN VEGETABLE MUFFINS

2 cups all-purpose flour
2 tablespoons sugar
1 tablespoon baking powder
¼ teaspoon salt
1 package (3 ounces) cream cheese
¾ cup milk
½ cup finely shredded or grated carrots
¼ cup chopped green onions
¼ cup vegetable oil
1 egg

1. Preheat oven to 400°F. Grease 12 (2½-inch) muffin cups or line with paper baking cups.

2. Combine flour, sugar, baking powder and salt in large bowl. Cut in cream cheese with pastry blender until coarse crumbs form.

3. Combine milk, carrots, green onions, oil and egg in small bowl until blended. Stir into flour mixture just until moistened. Spoon evenly into prepared muffin cups.

4. Bake 25 to 30 minutes until golden brown and toothpick inserted in center comes out clean.

5. Immediately remove from pan. Cool on wire rack about 10 minutes. Serve warm. *Makes 12 muffins*

DILLY CHEESE MUFFINS

2 cups all-purpose flour
1 tablespoon sugar
1 tablespoon baking powder
2 teaspoons dried dill weed
1 teaspoon onion powder
½ teaspoon salt
¼ teaspoon black pepper
1 cup creamed small curd cottage cheese
¾ cup milk
¼ cup butter, melted
1 egg, beaten

1. Preheat oven to 400°F. Grease 12 (2½-inch) muffin cups or line with paper baking cups. Combine flour, sugar, baking powder, dill weed, onion powder, salt and pepper in large bowl.

2. Combine cottage cheese, milk, butter and egg in small bowl until blended; stir into flour mixture just until moistened. Spoon into muffin cups.

3. Bake 20 to 25 minutes until light brown and toothpick inserted into centers come out clean. Remove from pan. Cool on wire rack.

Makes 12 muffins

PUMPERNICKEL MUFFINS

1 cup all-purpose flour
½ cup rye flour
½ cup whole-wheat flour
2 teaspoons caraway seeds
1 teaspoon baking soda
½ teaspoon salt
1 cup buttermilk
¼ cup vegetable oil
¼ cup light molasses
1 egg
1 square (1 ounce) unsweetened chocolate, melted and cooled

1. Preheat oven to 400°F. Grease 12 (2½-inch) muffin cups or line with paper baking cups.

2. Combine flours, caraway seeds, baking soda and salt in large bowl.

3. Combine buttermilk, oil, molasses and egg in small bowl until blended. Stir in melted chocolate. Stir into flour mixture just until moistened. Spoon evenly into prepared muffin cups.

4. Bake 20 to 25 minutes until toothpick inserted in center comes out clean. Immediately remove from pan. Cool on wire rack about 10 minutes. Serve warm or at room temperature. Store at room temperature in tightly covered container up to 2 days. *Makes 12 muffins*

PUMPERNICKEL MUFFINS

SOUTHERN BISCUIT MUFFINS

2½ cups all-purpose flour
¼ cup sugar
1½ tablespoons baking powder
¾ cup (1½ sticks) cold butter, cut into small pieces
1 cup cold milk

1. Preheat oven to 400°F. Grease 12 (2½-inch) muffin cups. (These muffins brown better on the sides and bottoms when baked without paper baking cups.)

2. Combine flour, sugar and baking powder in large bowl. Cut in butter with pastry blender or two knives until mixture resembles coarse crumbs. Stir in milk just until flour mixture is moistened. Spoon evenly into prepared muffin cups.

3. Bake 20 minutes or until light brown. Remove from pan. Cool on wire rack.

Makes 12 muffins

Baking Tips

These muffins taste like baking powder biscuits and are very quick and easy to make. Serve them with jelly, jam or honey.

SOUTHERN BISCUIT MUFFIN

CHEESY HAM AND PEPPER MUFFINS

2½ cups all-purpose flour
3 tablespoons sugar
1 tablespoon baking powder
¼ teaspoon black pepper
1 cup milk
6 tablespoons vegetable oil
2 eggs, beaten
2 tablespoons Dijon mustard
¾ cup shredded Swiss cheese
¾ cup diced cooked ham
3 tablespoons chopped red or green bell pepper

1. Preheat oven to 400°F. Grease 12 (2½-inch) muffin cups or line with paper baking cups.

2. Combine flour, sugar, baking powder and black pepper in large bowl. Whisk together milk, oil, eggs and mustard in small bowl until blended. Stir into flour mixture just until moistened. Fold in cheese, ham and bell pepper. Spoon evenly into prepared muffin cups.

3. Bake 19 to 21 minutes or until toothpick inserted into centers comes out clean. Cool in muffin pan on wire rack 5 minutes. Remove from pan and cool on wire rack 10 minutes. *Makes 12 muffins*

Variation: You can vary the taste of these muffins by substituting ¾ cup shredded Monterey Jack cheese with jalapeños or Cheddar cheese in place of the Swiss cheese.

CHEESY HAM AND PEPPER MUFFINS

RAISIN RICE BRAN MUFFINS

1¼ cups whole-wheat flour
¾ cup rice bran
¾ cup raisins
½ cup sugar
2 teaspoons baking powder
1 teaspoon ground cinnamon
½ teaspoon salt
1¼ cups buttermilk
3 tablespoons vegetable oil
2 egg whites, lightly beaten
Vegetable cooking spray

Combine flour, bran, raisins, sugar, baking powder, cinnamon, and salt in large bowl. Combine buttermilk, oil, and egg whites in small bowl; add to dry ingredients. Stir just until dry ingredients are moistened. Spoon batter into 12 muffin cups coated with cooking spray. Bake at 400°F. for 15 to 17 minutes. Cool slightly on wire rack. Serve warm.   *Makes 12 muffins*

Tip: Muffins may be stored in the freezer in freezer bag or tightly sealed container. To reheat frozen muffins, microwave each muffin on HIGH 30 to 40 seconds or heat at 350°F. for 12 to 15 minutes.

Favorite recipe from **USA Rice**

RAISIN RICE BRAN MUFFIN

POTATO PARMESAN MUFFINS

1 medium COLORADO potato, peeled and coarsely chopped
½ cup water
¼ cup milk
1⅔ cups all-purpose flour
3 tablespoons sugar
2 tablespoons grated Parmesan cheese, divided
2 teaspoons baking powder
½ teaspoon dried basil leaves
¼ teaspoon baking soda
¼ cup vegetable oil
1 egg, beaten

In small saucepan cook potato in ½ cup water, covered, over medium heat about 10 minutes or until tender. *Do not drain.* Mash until smooth or place mixture in blender container and blend until smooth. Add enough milk to measure 1 cup. In mixing bowl, combine flour, sugar, cheese, baking powder, basil and baking soda. Mix well. Combine potato mixture, oil and beaten egg; add all at once to flour mixture. Stir just until moistened. Spoon into greased or paper-lined muffin cups. Bake at 400°F for 20 minutes or until lightly browned. Remove from pan and cool on wire rack.

Makes 10 muffins

*Favorite recipe from **Colorado Potato Administrative Committee***

WISCONSIN BLUE CHEESE MUFFINS

2 cups all-purpose flour
3 tablespoons sugar
1 tablespoon baking powder
¼ teaspoon salt
1 cup Wisconsin Blue cheese, crumbled
1 egg, beaten
1 cup milk
¼ cup (½ stick) butter, melted

Preheat oven to 400°F. Butter 10 (2½-inch) muffin cups.

Combine flour, sugar, baking powder, salt and cheese in large bowl. Combine egg, milk and butter in small bowl until blended; stir into flour mixture just until moistened. Spoon into prepared muffin cups, filling ¾ full.

Bake 20 to 25 minutes or until golden brown. Remove from pan. Serve warm.

Makes 10 muffins

Favorite recipe from **Wisconsin Milk Marketing Board**

HAM AND CHEESE CORN MUFFINS

1 package (about 8 ounces) corn muffin mix
½ cup chopped deli ham
½ cup (2 ounces) shredded Swiss cheese
⅓ cup reduced-fat (2%) milk
1 egg
1 tablespoon Dijon mustard

1. Preheat oven to 400°F. Line 9 (2¾-inch) muffin cups with paper baking cups.

2. Combine muffin mix, ham and cheese in medium bowl. Beat milk, egg and mustard in 1-cup glass measure. Stir milk mixture into dry ingredients; mix just until moistened.

3. Fill muffin cups two-thirds full with batter. Bake 18 to 20 minutes or until light brown. Remove muffin pan to cooling rack. Let stand 5 minutes. Serve warm. *Makes 9 muffins*

Serving Suggestion: For added flavor, serve Ham and Cheese Corn Muffins with honey-flavored butter. To prepare, stir together equal amounts of honey and softened butter.

Prep Time: 10 minutes
Bake Time: 18 to 22 minutes

HAM AND CHEESE CORN MUFFINS

SPICED BROWN BREAD MUFFINS

2 cups whole wheat flour
⅔ cup all-purpose flour
⅔ cup packed brown sugar
2 teaspoons baking soda
1 teaspoon pumpkin pie spice*
2 cups buttermilk
¾ cup raisins

*Substitute ½ teaspoon ground cinnamon, ¼ teaspoon ground ginger and ⅛ teaspoon each ground allspice and ground nutmeg for 1 teaspoon pumpkin pie spice.

1. Preheat oven to 350°F. Grease 6 jumbo (4-inch) muffin cups.

2. Combine flours, sugar, baking soda and pumpkin pie spice in large bowl. Stir in buttermilk just until flour mixture is moistened. Fold in raisins. Spoon into muffin cups.

3. Bake 35 to 40 minutes or until toothpick inserted in center comes out clean. Remove from pan.   *Makes 6 jumbo muffins*

SPICED BROWN BREAD MUFFIN

Acknowledgments

The publisher would like to thank the companies and organizations listed below for the use of their recipes and photographs in this publication.

California Dried Plum Board

California Tree Fruit Agreement

Cherry Marketing Institute

Colorado Potato Administrative Committee

Crisco is a registered trademark of The J.M. Smucker Company

Dole Food Company, Inc.

Duncan Hines® and Moist Deluxe® are registered trademarks of Pinnacle Foods Corp.

EAGLE BRAND®

Equal® sweetener

Grandma's® is a registered trademark of Mott's, LLP

The Hershey Company

Jif® trademark of The J.M. Smucker Company

© Mars, Incorporated 2006

National Honey Board

Nestlé USA

SPLENDA® is a trademark of McNeil Nutritionals, LLC

Sun•Maid® Growers of California

Unilever

USA Rice Federation

Washington Apple Commission

Watkins Incorporated

Wisconsin Milk Marketing Board

Index

METRIC CONVERSION CHART

VOLUME MEASUREMENTS (dry)

$^1/_8$ teaspoon = 0.5 mL
$^1/_4$ teaspoon = 1 mL
$^1/_2$ teaspoon = 2 mL
$^3/_4$ teaspoon = 4 mL
1 teaspoon = 5 mL
1 tablespoon = 15 mL
2 tablespoons = 30 mL
$^1/_4$ cup = 60 mL
$^1/_3$ cup = 75 mL
$^1/_2$ cup = 125 mL
$^2/_3$ cup = 150 mL
$^3/_4$ cup = 175 mL
1 cup = 250 mL
2 cups = 1 pint = 500 mL
3 cups = 750 mL
4 cups = 1 quart = 1 L

VOLUME MEASUREMENTS (fluid)

1 fluid ounce (2 tablespoons) = 30 mL
4 fluid ounces ($^1/_2$ cup) = 125 mL
8 fluid ounces (1 cup) = 250 mL
12 fluid ounces (1$^1/_2$ cups) = 375 mL
16 fluid ounces (2 cups) = 500 mL

WEIGHTS (mass)

$^1/_2$ ounce = 15 g
1 ounce = 30 g
3 ounces = 90 g
4 ounces = 120 g
8 ounces = 225 g
10 ounces = 285 g
12 ounces = 360 g
16 ounces = 1 pound = 450 g

DIMENSIONS

$^1/_{16}$ inch = 2 mm
$^1/_8$ inch = 3 mm
$^1/_4$ inch = 6 mm
$^1/_2$ inch = 1.5 cm
$^3/_4$ inch = 2 cm
1 inch = 2.5 cm

OVEN TEMPERATURES

250°F = 120°C
275°F = 140°C
300°F = 150°C
325°F = 160°C
350°F = 180°C
375°F = 190°C
400°F = 200°C
425°F = 220°C
450°F = 230°C

BAKING PAN SIZES

Utensil	Size in Inches/Quarts	Metric Volume	Size in Centimeters
Baking or Cake Pan (square or rectangular)	8×8×2	2 L	20×20×5
	9×9×2	2.5 L	23×23×5
	12×8×2	3 L	30×20×5
	13×9×2	3.5 L	33×23×5
Loaf Pan	8×4×3	1.5 L	20×10×7
	9×5×3	2 L	23×13×7
Round Layer Cake Pan	8×1½	1.2 L	20×4
	9×1½	1.5 L	23×4
Pie Plate	8×1¼	750 mL	20×3
	9×1¼	1 L	23×3
Baking Dish or Casserole	1 quart	1 L	—
	1½ quart	1.5 L	—
	2 quart	2 L	—